Educational Research:
Principles, Policies
and Practices

$6/2/2

4

£4·95.

EDUCATIONAL ANALYSIS
General Editors: Philip Taylor and Colin Richards

CONTEMPORARY ANALYSIS IN EDUCATION SERIES
General Editor: Philip Taylor

Contemporary Analysis in Education Series

Educational Research: Principles, Policies and Practices

Edited by
Marten Shipman

The Falmer Press
(A member of the Taylor & Francis Group)
London and Philadelphia

UK   The Falmer Press, Falmer House, Barcombe, Lewes, East Sussex, BN8 5DL

USA   The Falmer Press, Taylor & Francis Inc., 242 Cherry Street, Philadelphia, PA 19106-1906

First published 1985

Library of Congress Cataloging in Publication Data

Main entry under title:

Educational research.

(Contemporary Analysis in Education Series)
1. Education—Research—Great Britain—Addresses, essays, lectures. I. Shipman, M. D. II. Series.
LB1028.E3186 1985 370′.7′8041 85-4585
ISBN 1-85000-027-1

Jacket design by Leonard Williams

Typeset in 11/13 Garamond by
Imago Publishing Ltd, Thame, Oxon.

Printed in Great Britain by Taylor & Francis (Printers) Ltd, Basingstoke

Contents

General Editor's Preface

Educational research has proliferated in recent years. It engages more people, consumes more resources and commands more attention than was the case a quarter of a century ago. It is also vastly more disparate in methodology and sophisticated in presentation. Rarely are simple remedies offered to complex problems. The computer, that easy manipulator of data, that effortless number cruncher has been put in its place as one among an array of tools for research into education. It is this that this collection of papers shows.

Marten Shipman has provided a substantive conspectus of the field and his fellow contributors have filled this out. Theirs may not be the last word but theirs is as valuable an introduction to the nature of educational research in the latter part of the twentieth century as any currently available.

Educational research will continue to evolve, to vary its 'attack' on the many problems which confront teachers and administrators but it will not go away. It is this that this volume finally affirms: educational research is here to stay.

Philip Taylor
Birmingham

Editor's Introduction

Most social researchers nurse a frustration. The solutions to the problems they uncover usually lie deep in the structure of society. Radical political action seems to be required to effect beneficial changes. But no such action is likely and those who recommend it are likely to lose support. That is the lot of many educational researchers. Throughout the articles that follow there is that hidden, frustrating agenda. Yet one ongoing responsibility of educational researchers is to produce regular reminders that old injustices persist while new ones are uncovered.

In the 1950s it was exciting to show that class inequality was rife in education, just as it is to show gender injustice in the 1980s. But, one after another, newly uncovered trends can be left to 'maintenance' research. It is a crucial task of researchers to remind us that resources, opportunities and the potential for benefiting one's children are distributed with neither justice nor reason. But such reminders need less investment once the message has been learned by those who develop policies and practise them.

Most of the researchers contributing to this book are concerned with the way research is organized to investigate the processes through which identifiable groups come to be penalized in schools. They have a particular concern with the parallel trends towards interpretive research methods and to the involvement of teachers in research as a form of professional development. These have both accelerated in the last twenty years. They are closely related, for interpretive research based on observation appears more practicable for teachers because it needs fewer resources than experiments or surveys and is focused on the here and now. But the methodological issues in these trends are of urgent concern. The ease with which quantitative approaches can be criticized and the relative insulation from the critical scalpel of the qualitative researcher not only reinforces each trend by reducing the risk involved, but makes the examination of the logic of the methods more urgent. That is a major theme of this book and the particular concern of Atkinson and Delamont, and Adelman and Young.

The trends also challenge the status of educational and other human science. While the paramount methods were those of the natural sciences a claim could be sustained to scientific status as it was publicly understood. As the ethnographic, ethogenic, phenomenological, interpretive attack has been launched in one social science after another, the resulting research doesn't look scientific to the public, regardless of the sophistication of the definitions of social science used in the various academic communities. The Economic and Social Research Council, without the Science in the previous SSRC title it replaced, is an indicator of this view of the change in status as the imperfections of scientistic social science were stressed by those involved. It may have been the direct result of Sir Keith Joseph's interest in the philosophy of science, but the evidence had been presented to him by those who were most affected.

Within education, this change in status has an additional significance. Qualitative research seems to be about observations that are the stock-in-trade of teachers, advisers and inspectors. Adelman and Young stress the importance of the accounts of those involved, yet point to the rarity of their inclusion in interpretive research reports. Atkinson and Delamont stress that case study research remains a dead-end because no base in theory has been developed to guide the steady accumulation of evidence. These accounts can also be used to challenge the standing of research when it contradicts that produced by others who work in the classrooms observed, who know the children intimately, or have experience of inspecting and advising teachers.

There has, however, been a considerable gain from the focus on the processes within education and the involvement of practitioners alongside researchers. We now know more about the processes in schools that account for the different attainments of different groups. More importantly, we now know more about the impact of factors within school and classroom that can be managed by teachers. This has removed much of the determinism that marked both psychological and sociological explanations up to 1970. Innate and unchangeable intelligence was as closed to remedial action as deprived cultural backgrounds and inadequate families. Genetic and social engineering are not expected of teachers. The factors observed in the classroom are, however, within the province of teaching. This has brought a usefulness to research that partially compensates for the more exposed status of the qualitative researcher who produces it and for the difficulties in building coherence into separate case studies.

The book moves from the recent history of educational research detailed by myself and Edgar Stones, through the problems raised by changing methods in Part 1, to the impact on policies and practices, and to ways of increasing effectiveness in Part 2. Each of the contributors has been actively engaged, either as researcher, or as a user of the evidence produced. Each is concerned with increasing the information available for decision-making, whether through advancing the theories that aid understanding, or the reliability of the evidence produced.

Finally, many of the chapters that follow are concerned with the change from empirical to interpretive research. In Part 1 this concern is with the organization of the research enterprise in Education and the methodological issues, as observation, case study, illuminative evaluation, ethnography have become popular at the expense of experiment, survey, test-based assessment and statistical treatment of data. The benefit of this shift of emphasis has been in the rejection of the determinism built into methods derived from the natural sciences. Qualitative methods are aimed at uncovering meanings and emphasize the variability of human response, not its conditioning. In Part 2 the concern is with the impact of research on policy and again with the implications of the switch to qualitative methods that lack the apparent scientistic quality of experiment, survey and comparison.

1
Educational Research: Principles and Policies

Developments in Educational Research

Marten Shipman

Introduction

In this Chapter the organization of educational research in Britain and the recent changes in methods and their justification are reviewed. Across the quarter of the century from 1960 there have been developments that have affected the nature of the evidence made available to decision-makers in classroom, county and town hall and central government. Even more important, there is a close link between the organization of the research enterprise, the logic behind the methods used and the evidence. It is useful to review the changes as an introduction to the issues raised by researchers and users of research that follow. But it is essential to examine the theoretical assumptions underlying educational research for these have changed to reveal new perspectives and old prejudices.

Five closely related developments lie behind the educational research enterprise in the late 1980s. First, it has become an established part of the education service. Second, it has attained some independence from the human sciences that controlled it in the 1960s. Third, it has nevertheless been disturbed by the disputes over the status of knowledge within those sciences. Fourth, educational research has been moved out of academia to become part of wider professional activity involving collaborative and school-based activity, with consequent problems of status. Fifth, research designed to produce accounts of the meanings of situations from those investigated, has uncovered the assumptions behind earlier research of a quantitative, top-down design and shown that it was in practice producing a white, anglo-saxon, male view of the educational world.

The Establishment of Educational Research

There was a promise about education in the 1960s that has to be considered alongside rising numbers in schools to account for the extra investment that was made. It was seen as a key to economic prosperity and to greater social equality. There may now be disillusionment alongside falling rolls in the 1980s, but investment in research was seen as a central part of the drive to use education to create a more prosperous and just society. The contemporary research enterprise has to be seen in the context of changes in that climate for education. What is striking is not the shrinking of research across the quarter of a century, but its health amid a jaundiced service.

The increase in scale of educational research in the 1960s and 1970s was rapid. Organizations devoted to, or employing researchers, proliferated. The most significant was the establishment of the Social Science Research Council in 1965 by a Royal Charter spelling out responsibilities to support and carry out research, and to fund postgraduate instruction in the social sciences. An Educational Research Board was set up alongside committees for other social sciences. Even with major cuts in resources, the Education and Human Development Committee of the renamed Economic and Social Research Council was supporting some eighty projects in 1984 (ESRC, 1984). It had drawn up *Priorities for Research* (ESRC, 1983) and was initiating as well as responding to them.

A list of organizations initiating and funding educational research gives a flavour of the increased scale from 1960. Schools Council from 1964, the Educational Disadvantage Unit, the National Council for Educational Technology, the Inner London Education Authority's Research and Statistics Group all date as research enterprises from this period. Even more striking has been the increased involvement of the Department of Education and Science. This started on a significant scale with the Educational Priority Area Projects following the Plowden Report (1967). The Department not only remains the largest source of supply for funding research, but through the Assessment of Performance Unit supplies a major part of the money available to the National Foundation for Educational Research. The decision to provide support for educational research was only made by the Minister of Education in 1961. Since then it has moved, as has the Social Science Research Council, from responding to initiatives from outside, to commissioning work of direct relevance. But, like other government departments, particularly the

Department of Health and Social Security, it remains the paymaster for a major part of the relevant research enterprise.

Across the 1960s and 1970s there was also an increase in the resources made available from public and private bodies. The Nuffield Foundation invested heavily in curriculum development in the early 1960s and remains an important source of funds for contemporary research into developments such as graded testing. The budgets of the National Foundation for Educational Research in England, the Scottish Council for Research in Education and the Northern Ireland Council for Educational Research increased. Above all, the sources of funds widened. The prospective educational researcher can approach the Rowntree Trust, Leverhulme, Nuffield, and so on with confidence that education is seen as an established area for funding. That acceptance has come in the last two decades.

The Independence of Educational Researchers

In 1960, the small contingent of educational researchers were mostly trained and working as psychologists or sociologists. There were no books published in this country on specifically educational research methods. An organization such as the British Educational Research Association described in Chapter 2 by Stones would have been inconceivable. Twenty years on the organization exists, the research methods books proliferate and contemporary researchers have often trained as specifically educational experts outside the more established social science communities. This establishment of an independent educational research community has been rapid. Many still work within the theoretical frameworks from psychology, sociology and so on, but there are others, often young, who have not been inducted into these external references for investigating education. The very different allegiances pervade the contributions to this book. They produce not only different issues for investigation, but contrasting interpretations of the same features.

The negative reason for the establishment of a specifically educational research enterprise is the continuing conflict within the social sciences. This is well documented for Sociology where a leading figure such as Gouldner (1980) can maintain that it is necessary to insist on its contradictory, unsatisfactory and uncertain nature as a condition for understanding its potential. In Psychology the conflict has been more muted, but it has still been radical, thrusting at the assumptions about mechanistic models of humanity at the heart of the established discipline (Harre and Secord, 1972). With the certainty of functionalism or Marxism within Sociology and of behaviourism within Psychology disintegrating, there was an incentive to emigrate to the new shores of Education as a distinctive community.

The positive reasons for the emergence of an educational research community lie in the expansion across the 1960s and 1970s that brought resources, employment, publicity and promotion. All departments expanded and there was a growing market for publication. Training in research methods became a part of proliferating Masters programmes in education departments. This has produced a generation identifying with Education as a discipline in its own right, not as a subject for enquiry within another established social science.

The expanding research community in departments within universities became more specialized and differentiated in the 1970s. First, the specifically educational subject areas were concentrated. The curriculum, heavily funded by the Schools Council, became a specialism of the Centre for Applied Research in Education at East Anglia. The management of learning in classrooms was concentrated at Lancaster under Bennett as Professor of Educational Research and at Leicester under Galton as co-director of the ORACLE project. School studies became a speciality at Sussex with Lacey and at Oxford with Hargreaves. This concentration was encouraged by the policy of the Educational Research Board of the Social Science Research Council which selected outlets for training awards and concentrated research contracts in centres of excellence. Similarly Assessment of Performance Unit contracts went to specialist centres for science at Chelsea College and the University of Leeds.

There is an obvious age difference in the degree of independence from established social sciences among educational researchers. Thus Lacey's work on Hightown Grammar (Lacey, 1970) started within the Department of Social Anthropology at Manchester in 1960. Lacey (1976) has described the influences on the design of that pioneering school study. Twenty years later Ball published *Beachside Comprehensive* (1981) and has described his methodological apprenticeship at Sussex where Lacey was his supervisor (Ball, 1984). The conceptual context has changed along with the clientele in the respective departments. By the end of the period there were hopes for a genuine, applicable science of teaching and learning developed by educational researchers (Bennett, 1979). Furthermore, many influential studies owed little to psychology or sociology and were focused on the management of learning in the classroom after investigating how this was organized as a basis for suggesting ways in which it could be improved (for example, Bennett *et al*, 1984, Galton and Willcocks, 1983 and Stones, 1984).

The Status of the Knowledge-Base for Education

The decreased dependence on established social sciences in educational research is a mirror of the reorganization of courses in Education within teacher education and in-service courses. The central roles for the Sociology of, the Psychology of, Education have been replaced by more professionally orientated work that uses the social sciences, but is more pedagogical in approach. Teaching and research have moved away from the confident use of psychological and sociological evidence as its limitations have been exposed (Shipman, 1981). However, the logic behind the methods, the methodology of research, is closely related to the theoretical positions adopted. Acknowledging conflicts within the social sciences does not only affect the status of evidence, it raises questions about the ways it has been collected.

Within Sociology, for example, there has been a dramatic swing from functionalism where the emphasis was on the coherence of institutions to phenomenological perspectives where the focus is on the meanings of events to those involved. This has not only produced a swing from surveys to observational studies. It has produced radical changes in the approach to research (Bulmer and Burgess, 1981 and Bogdan and Biklen, 1982). As radicals attacked the use of natural science methods that assumed a passive, unthinking human as subject, they destroyed much of the base of evidence that had served decision-makers, particularly in teacher education.

There were problems for the expert in this demolition. It showed the fallibility of theories about human attainment, personality, development and variety. The imposition of categories onto human behaviour gave it a predictability, a dependent, determined character that was against common sense when applied to as complex a phenomenon as intelligence. Lay people were right that it was not fixed at birth, was affected by the environment, could not be measured accurately. When this concept's dependence on invalid tests was exposed, the psychologists lost prestige. Similarly sociologists could no longer speak about cultural deprivation with authority once the focus of interest switched to the meanings given to situations, for these illustrated the variety of ways of life and the riches among the apparent poverty. The evidence of the 1960s is not just laughable twenty five years later, it is a public warning against any dogma among the experts. The sad story of Sir Cyril Burt (Hearnshaw, 1979) is a warning against claiming to be authoritative.

The Status of Educational Research

As the numbers involved in educational research have increased and as the thesis, dissertation and long essay on higher degrees join the professional research report, so the gap between producer and consumer has narrowed. Furthermore, many researchers have intentionally promoted a collaborative, school-based enterprise. The Centre for Applied Research in Education under the influence of Stenhouse has been the launch pad of much of this work. The Humanities Curriculum Project (Elliott and MacDonald, 1975), The Ford Teaching Project, the Teacher–Pupil Interaction and Quality of Learning (TIQL) and the Cambridge Accountability Project all spring from the belief in involving teachers in investigating their own professional behaviour. The last three have been directed by Elliott (1975, 1981a and 1981b). Elliott also established the Classroom Action Research Network. Stones describes the growth of the British Educational Research Association in Chapter 2. But alongside this primarily academic body grew the Association for the Study of the Curriculum which unites teachers and researchers in one of many such bodies. Further opportunities for collaborative activity to promote greater awareness of the potential of research have been organized around data such as that at the University of Edinburgh under McPherson (see, for example, Gray, McPherson and Raffe, 1983). This archive is made available to teachers, administrators and inspectors to extract the information required and to carry out their own research. Finally, there has been a remarkable increase of research activity centred on teacher self-assessment, in-school evaluation, curriculum development and in-service training.

The merging of research into professional development has been rapid. Indeed, research is now a normal part of work in schools and colleges. For the professional researcher this is a triumph. But the cost has been high. The audience are more knowing and can criticize from their own experience. The expansion has exposed the social limits of growth. When educational researchers were few they were promoted rapidly. They were accorded prestige because they offered a rare package. Now they congregate in hundreds and promotion is unlikely. The involvement of teachers and others in research also reduces the scarcity value of research evidence. *Social Relations in a Secondary School* (Hargreaves, 1967) was a bestseller. Now school studies may drag. There is a boundary problem, not only because many are engaged in doing research, but because ethnography brings the researcher close to the journalist. The publication of a school case study may be of intense interest to the media (Ball, 1984). This boundary problem is the price paid for the interest raised. The esoteric is safest for the recluse. Exerting influence and promoting professionality in a large scale enterprise such as the education service not only brings the glare of publicity, but exposes researchers to familiarity.

The Exposure of Assumptions

Research methods, the data collected and the theories which are verified or generated are inseparable. But the relation between them has often been neglected. When psychologists and sociologists used the experimental and survey methods of the natural sciences to investigate human behaviour they were working with theories that yielded the concepts and categories that guided the research. This was top-down because the concern was with models of intelligence or learning, socialization and social control rather than with the way the individual subjects made sense of their world. Once phenomenological, interpretive approaches became more popular, there was not just a fashion for observational studies to get at the meanings from the individual's viewpoint. That search for meanings uncovered assumptions in the concepts, categories and methods. Often the concepts used such as social class, motivation or culture were shown to lead to views on the poor or the minorities that were misleading and insulting once their interpretations were taken into account. The most alarming revelation was the sex bias in social research.

The best illustration of the way the conceptual frameworks and methods in use produced evidence from a male viewpoint has come in Sociology. Women were invisible, rarely the subject of investigation (Stacey, 1981). Yet the assumptions made about them influenced the way investigations were made and information collected even into official statistics (Oakley and Oakley, 1979). It is now argued that it is not just necessary to undertake research about women, but to do feminist research, that is to adopt an approach that puts women first (Oakley, 1981). This is a challenge to the way research has been male biased. The flavour of this remarkable development can be got from two recent titles, *Doing Feminist Research* (Roberts, 1981) and *Breaking Out: Feminist Consciousness and Feminist Research* (Stanley and Wise, 1981).

The new visibility of women in research serves to underline the importance of the connection between methods and the theories that are the sources of hypotheses and the basis for interpreting data. It has even been possible to re-interpret completed research from a feminist viewpoint (Morgan, 1981). Women are becoming visible in research and the world from their viewpoint is being explored. The Social Science Research Council for example funded research to repeat the work of Willis in *Learning to Labour* (1977) and this has shown a world for young women after leaving school that is very different from their brothers (Griffin, 1982). Unfortunately, such differences were often ignored in educational research. The breakthrough came with the switch to qualitative methods informed by phenomenology with its emphasis on how people made sense of the world around them. In a brief period feminist research has not just revealed this very different reality, but has exposed the bias in previous evidence.

The lesson from the invisibility of women in social scientific research has to be remembered throughout. This did not come from only the superficial use of categories and definitions that were male orientated. Underlying methods are theories and concepts. These may be explicit in subjects such as Psychology or Sociology. They may be implicit, a set of unexamined assumptions lying behind the way research is conceived and executed. But in all cases, including qualitative, ethnographic research, those assumptions influence the evidence produced through their impact on design, execution and interpretation. This applies to educational research, even when the focus is on descriptions of life in classrooms or on pedagogy. The practice of ethnography has gone faster than thinking about its phenomenological, interactionist, ethnomethodological justification. The gap is slowly being closed by discussions of the role of theory (see, for example, Hammersley and Atkinson, 1983, and Atkinson and Delamont in this book). Until that closure occurs the danger remains that the next generation will show us that we unintentionally overlooked important issues and biased those we did investigate.

References

BALL, S.J. (1981) *Beachside Comprehensive: A Case Study of Secondary Schooling*, Cambridge, Cambridge University Press.

BALL, S.J. (1984) 'Beachside reconsidered: reflections on a methodological apprenticeship', in BURGESS, R.G. (Ed.), *The Research Process in Educational Settings: Ten Case Studies*, Lewes, Falmer Press.

BENNETT, S.N. (1979) 'Recent research on teaching: a dream, a belief, and a model' in BENNETT, S.N. and MCNAMARA, D. (Eds.) *Focus on Teaching*, London, Longman.

BENNETT, S.N. *et al* (1984) *The Quality of Pupil Learning Experiences*, Hillsdale N.J., L. Erlbaum.

BOGDAN, R. and BIKLEN, S.K. (1982) *Qualitative Research for Education: An Introduction to Theory and Methods*, Boston, Allyn and Bacon.

BULMER, M. and BURGESS, R.G. (1981) *Sociology*, 15, 4, (Special Issue), British Sociological Association.

ECONOMIC AND SOCIAL RESEARCH COUNCIL (1983) *Priorities for Research*, Education and Human Development Committee, London, ESRC.

ECONOMIC AND SOCIAL RESEARCH COUNCIL, (1984) *Newsletter*, 52, p. 23, London, ESRC.

ELLIOTT, J. (1975) *Ford Teaching Project Units*, Cambridge, Cambridge Institute of Education.

ELLIOTT, J. (1981a) *Teacher–Pupil Interaction and the Quality of Learning*, TIQL memo no. 1, Cambridge, Cambridge Institute of Education.

ELLIOTT, J. (1981b) *Cambridge Accountability Project; Case Studies in School Accountability*, Cambridge, Cambridge Institute of Education.

ELLIOTT, J. and MACDONALD, B. (1975) *People in Classrooms*, Occasional Paper 2, University of East Anglia, Centre for Applied Research in Education.

GALTON, M. and WILLCOCKS, J. (1983) *Moving from the Primary Classroom*, London, Routledge and Kegan Paul.

GOULDNER, A.W. (1980) *The Two Marxisms*, London, Macmillan.

GRAY, J., MCPHERSON, A.F. and RAFFE, D. (1983) *Reconstructions of Secondary Education*, London, Routledge and Kegan Paul.

GRIFFIN, C. (1982) *The Good, the Bad and the Ugly: Images of Young Women in the Labour Market*, Birmingham, Centre for Contemporary Cultural Studies, stencilled paper.

HAMMERSLEY, M. and ATKINSON, P. (1983) *Ethnography: Principles and Practice*, London, Tavistock.

HARGREAVES, D.H. (1967) *Social Relations in a Secondary School*, London, Routledge and Kegan Paul.

HARRE, R. and SECORD, P.F. (1972) *The Explanation of Human Behaviour*, Oxford, Blackwell.

HEARNSHAW, L.S. (1979) *Cyril Burt, Psychologist*, London, Hodder and Stoughton.

LACEY, C. (1970) *Hightown Grammar*, Manchester, Manchester University Press.

LACEY, C. (1976) 'Problems of sociological fieldwork: a review of the methodology of "Hightown Grammar",' in SHIPMAN, M. (Ed.) *The*

Organization and Impact of Social Research, London, Routledge and Kegan Paul.

MORGAN, D.H. (1981) 'Men, masculinity and the process of sociological enquiry', in ROBERTS, H., *Doing Feminist Research*, London, Routledge and Kegan Paul.

OAKLEY, A. (1981) 'Interviewing women: a contradiction in terms', in ROBERTS, H. (Ed.) *Doing Feminist Research*, London, Routledge and Kegan Paul.

OAKLEY, A. and OAKLEY, R. (1979) 'Sexism in official statistics', in IRVINE, J. *et al*, *Demystifying Social Statistics*, London, Pluto.

PLOWDEN REPORT (1967) *Children and their Primary Schools*, London, HMSO.

ROBERTS, H. (1981) *Doing Feminist Research*, London, Routledge and Kegan Paul.

SHIPMAN, M. (1981) *The Limitations of Social Research* (2nd Ed.), London, Longman.

STACEY, M. (1981) 'The division of labour revisited or overcoming the two Adams', in ABRAMS, P. *et al.*, *Practice and Progress: British Sociology 1950–1980*, London, Allen and Unwin.

STANLEY, L. and WISE, S. (1983) *Breaking Out: Feminist Consciousness and Feminist Research*, London, Routledge and Kegan Paul.

STONES, E. (1984) *Supervision in Teacher Education: A Counselling and Pedagogical Approach*, London, Methuen.

WILLIS, P. (1977) *Learning to Labour*, Farnborough, Saxon House.

The Development of the British Educational Research Association: A Personal View

Edgar Stones

At one of the planning meetings of the *ad hoc* committee when we were agonizing about the name of the new organization some wag suggested BERO. It was a more apt title than many realized at the time because whatever else it became, at that time it was certainly self-raising.

The origins of the Association go back to the sixties. At the time research in education was struggling to escape from the dominant psychometric paradigm that leaned heavily on psychology and the testing movement. Educational research had for some time virtually connoted the development of ever more sophisticated statistical methods of measuring people, especially in connection with selection for secondary education, and the NFER was for years predominantly a test production agency. In the second half of the decade research in other fields of educational studies began to develop, but as far as BERA is concerned I believe that it was the development of classroom studies that brought to a focus work in the various fields and led to the perceived need for an interdisciplinary forum of the nature of BERA.

Classroom Studies

Probably the earliest gathering to discuss classroom studies was held at Lancaster in 1970. The initiator was John Garner, a member of the Department of Educational Research at the University who circulated educational institutions inviting interested people to contact him. From the start the group was interdisciplinary which, together with the focus on a relatively unexplored field, engaged and enthused participants. After the second meeting John left for Australia and Sara Delamont took over the organizing of seminars and the numbers of those interested grew from fewer than twenty at the outset to about eighty in 1973. In that year Ned Flanders was temporarily imported to join the seminar which was funded by SSRC.

In 1972 the present author organized a seminar on research in teacher education on behalf of the Committee for Research into Teacher Education. This group included many from the Classroom Studies group and was followed by a second seminar on the same topic funded by SSRC. The interesting thing about these gatherings was that people with similar interests from different disciplinary backgrounds were coming together for the first time. Indeed, many well known to each other by publications had never actually met. It was this coming together of people from varied disciplinary backgrounds in informal stimulating discussion that provided the context and the impetus for the birth of BERA.

Conception

Conception was leisurely and extended over several informal discussions between the present author and Brian Start then of the NFER. We thought that the contacts established and the discussions started should be encouraged and made permanent by some form of formal structure. At the same time we wanted to preserve the interactive nature of the discussions we had enjoyed in the *ad hoc* meetings and to avoid the set piece, large scale, one way traffic encounters of which we felt there were enough at that time. We had in mind the model of AERA and in 1973 we discussed the question with colleagues we thought might be interested. We decided to approach the DES for a small subvention as a pump primer to get together people who might help to start the proposed association. Shortly afterwards Brian Start left to a chair in Australia and the DES refused the subvention. Despite these setbacks a meeting to discuss the formation of an association interested in research in education was held in Birmingham on 12 October 1973 and gestation commenced.

Gestation

This first meeting was convened and chaired by the present author and eighteen interested people attended. The meeting decided to make the attempt to form an association and agreed on the title *British Educational Research Association*. The nature of membership gave rise to much discussion and eventually it was decided that membership should be open. In the early stages the steering committee would run the Association and all original members agreed to submit the names of those they thought would be interested to the present author to compile a list of possible members. The aim was to obtain as wide a spread of subject interests as possible.

The main objective of the Association was to be the advancement of educational research in Britain. Subsidiary specific aims were the holding of national conferences and regional conferences, the publication of conference reports, bibliographical surveys, providing information on research tools and approaches. Arrangements were made to investigate the possibility of publications and to prepare a constitution. Attempts were to be made to secure a pump priming grant to get BERA off the ground (£10,000 was the target). An inaugural meeting was decided on to be held in Birmingham in the spring of 1974.

Soon after this meeting information was received that a European body similar to BERA was being discussed. A key issue concerning the people involved was the most appropriate nature of membership, should it be restricted to those actively engaged in research or open to all those interested? Although there may have been a certain conflict of interests between this projected body and BERA, the BERA planning committee thought it a minor problem and pressed on. As far as I am aware, this projected European association did not materialize but it was an interesting sign of contemporary concern and in fact national groupings such as BERA began to emerge in other countries in the years following its establishment.

During the rest of 1973 messages of support and expressions of interest were received and by the end of the year a list of about 200 possible members had been compiled from information received from members of the planning group by the present author who continued to act as convener and administrator. In December 1973 the planning group met again. It was reported that all efforts to secure a pump priming grant from various funding bodies had failed so that if BERA were to rise it would be a bootstrap operation. The main business of the meeting was the question of membership and the constitution. There was a very strong thread of opinion that argued for an element of professional organization to protect the interests of research workers who had (and have) very insecure career structures. The question of whether membership should be 'open', 'closed', or 'quasi-closed' again attracted much discussion. In the event it was decided that the overt espousal of a type of trade union stance on behalf of research workers was not the main concern of the projected association although all agreed it was an important issue. The question of 'open' versus 'closed' membership was resolved by the device of 'voting' and 'associate' membership, the former comprising the activists and the latter the interested.

Further meetings of the planning committee received more refusals to fund and produced a draft constitution to go to the inaugural conference. Prospective members were circulated inviting them to join and to attend the inaugural conference. The programme of the conference was agreed with the focus on problems of conducting research taking a multi-disciplinary approach.

Parturition

Delivery was relatively painless. The painstaking preparation of the planning committee paid off and even the adoption of the constitution went smoothly. Other business matters took decisions to announce the new arrival to kindred organizations, to aim for a regular 'occasional' publication of a multi-disciplinary nature and a newsletter, *Research Intelligence*.

The rest of the conference was devoted to papers and discussion and set an impressive precedent for future occasions. The keynote paper by John Nisbet on *Educational Research: the State of the Art* was a seminal contribution that not only provided a conspectus of the way things were then, but also delineated some possible future perspectives. Other papers considered the politics of funding of educational research, problems of methodology, and the audience for educational research. Two distinctive strands perhaps reflected the origins of the Association; they were on classroom studies and problems of evaluation (mainly related to curriculum).

After the inaugural conference the planning committee continued to meet, organized elections and set in train arrangements for implementing the decisions of Conference. It was decided to go for charitable status so that BERA's bootstrap operation would be untrammelled by tax problems. Publications and future conferences were discussed.

The year following, conferences reflecting two abiding interests of the Association were held, one on the training of research workers and the other on problems of research in teaching. The annual conference was held in Stirling and was well attended. *Research Intelligence* was published in mimeographed form as the journal of BERA and the Association's newsletter initially appeared as an appendix to communications from the secretary. In 1977 publication of the Association's journal was assumed by Carfax under the title *British Educational Research Journal* and the Association's newsletter continued under the style of *Research Intelligence*, as had been envisaged from the beginning.

Subsequent conferences and seminars have continued BERA's concern with classroom studies and careers of research workers. In 1979 a seminar on classroom studies was reported in a NFER publication *Understanding Classroom Life* (McAleese and Hamilton 1978). A more recent seminar on the supervision of research students in 1981 was reported by one of BERA's first independent publications (Eggleston and Delamont 1983). Another of these BERA publications fulfils the commitment on providing information on research tools; it is the list of British journals concerned with education (Vaughan 1983).

Thus at the time of writing (December 1983) at the end of the first decade of BERA's life, it would seem that the objectives of the founders have been met. Their early anxieties about whether the Association would be viable are now relieved and membership is growing steadily. Throughout the travails of birth and the neonatal years, however, midwifery support from funding bodies was notably missing. BERA was indeed 'self-raising' and its membership is now around 500.

Since the early debates about the nature of membership, the matter has been resolved further by the assimilation of the associate membership category to the voting category and the introduction of corporate membership for schools. There are, of course, still problems but the considerable difficulties of establishing the Association have been overcome and the ground is now laid for the further expansion of membership and enhancement of the service to members and the influence of BERA in the education and research community.

Currents, Swirls, and Eddies

When the editor invited me to write about BERA and make some comment about the currents of concerns that had preoccupied the Association, I replied that this was not too easy and rather than currents I perceived rather vague and confused swirls and eddies. It is probable that this hasty reply was not entirely accurate and I have already suggested two themes that have persisted and still attract a good deal of attention from BERA members.

In the very early days of the planning committee, the preponderance of people from the field of educational psychology caused some concern. Since the prime movers at the time were themselves of that persuasion the imbalance was not surprising but there was a very strong press to redress it. The focusing on topics such as the careers and training of research workers and on classroom studies had helped the development of a multi-disciplinary movement and the hegemony of the psychologists was gradually dissipated. The present author soon began to extend his vocabulary to include such topics as ethnomethodology and symbolic interactionism which may now be household words but were then arcane mysteries to unreconstructed empiricists such as me. Empiricism itself took a battering fairly early in the life of BERA, but despite the occasional tense moment in seminars when the knives flashed, the conflict has been creative and has induced a more thorough examination of fashionable shibboleths than would have been the case had BERA not existed.

After the empiricists graciously yielded prominence, sociologists quickly moved in with anthropologists and curriculum theorists lurking greyly on the fringes. Roving bands of feminists made sporadic raids and established redoubts that enjoyed total impregnability in the face of complete lack of opposition. Historians calmly observed with due disinterested detachment but unfortunately philosophers have been little observed. Perhaps in the next decade they will acknowledge that BERA does, indeed, exist and I, personally, look forward to their increased participation in its affairs.

Presidential addresses have reflected the diversity of concerns that characterize BERA. Following the general overview at the inaugural meeting (Nisbet 1974) topics have included a report on empirical investigations on conceptual learning in different ethnic groups (Stones 1975), on pitfalls in educational research (Wrigley 1976), critique of past educational research and indications for the future (Simon 1977), mapping the domain in educational research (Eggleston 1979), case and sample studies (Stenhouse 1980), is education getting better? (Choppin 1981), the application of research (Wragg 1982), democracy and pragmatism in educational research (Chambers 1983) and women's place in education (Delamont 1984).

Contributed papers have been at least as diverse as presidential addresses. Many have reported on specific research projects and it would be invidious to single out specific papers but some topics have been research into truancy, effects of pre-school experience, development of mathematical concepts in young children, research in language and reading, multi-racial education, special educational needs, ethics and evaluation and various aspects of the history of education. Although the heterogeneity may at times be thought to have led to a certain superficiality of treatment, this danger has been far outweighed by the effects of subjecting one's work to appraisal from colleagues outside one's immediate circle who are often able to bring fresh insights to bear on old problems.

In all conferences there have been symposia. Frequently these have addressed topics related to the conducting of research in education. For example seminars at several conferences considered problems of assessment in research. Dissemination and the organization and impact of research have also constituted an abiding preoccupation as has the question of resources for research.

Questions not directly related to problems of conducting research have appeared with some regularity. One, that perhaps reflects a certain ambivalence or unease of some researchers, has been a continuing debate about the role of teachers and schools in research: 'on' or 'together with', that is the question. There is little doubt where most members' hearts lie as is evidenced by the decision to admit schools only to corporate membership. Whether their minds will catch up in time to convince schools that BERA has something to offer them is, at the time of writing, unclear.

Classroom studies, teaching and pedagogy have also constituted a school related theme that has appeared with some regularity and continues the pre-BERA tradition. The place of computers in education and educational research attracts attention in most conferences and research in the history of education and the history of educational research are continuing themes which provide material of interest for all members whatever their specific subjects.

One of BERA's early objectives, to organize regional conferences and seminars, has been particularly fruitful. Seminars or 'mini-conferences' with the participation of between fifteen and thirty people have been held on such subjects as the training of research students, problems of research methodology, the place of women in educational research, research in classrooms and research into teaching, and in-service education. BERA organized what was probably the first demonstration of on-line interrogation of the ERIC system to a seminar, thus furthering one other of its early objectives.

Perhaps an undercurrent perceptible at annual conferences has been the concern with power and educational research. The device used by politicians and civil servants to fund projects likely to give post-hoc legitimacy to decisions already or about to be made has been referred to by more than one guest speaker. Christopher Price raised this issue and others concerned with the relationship between politics and educational research in a stimulating and sceptical address at the Nottingham conference in 1977. The same conference also saw some sharp questioning of the role of the DES and the SSRC in providing for educational research. The 1983 conference got a clear message from Denis Lawton when he said: ' . . . it is not enough to do good research, you must improve your public and professional image, and above all develop an organization with political influence' (Lawton 1983). BERA has not, however, been totally supine and oblivious to outside events. The President and Council supported the SSRC in the face of political attack and made sharp comment on the pseudo research of the so-called Centre for Policy Studies (*Research Intelligence*, 1981). It may be, however, that we were merely beating the air and that we need to put the developing of political influence on the agenda for the next decade of BERA's existence.

I think the omens are reasonably favourable for such a development. Despite cut-backs, redundancies and early retirement, membership is growing steadily, publications are reasonably well established, links with other learned societies in Britain and overseas are being made and in view of the cross-disciplinarity of the Association there is no reason why it should not build up a substantially increased membership in the next few years, a development that would provide a firmer foundation for the kind of development Lawton advocated.

References

CHAMBERS, P. (1983) 'Democratisation and pragmatism in educational research', *British Educational Research Journal*, 9, 1, pp. 3–6.

CHOPPIN, B. (1981) 'Is education getting better?', *British Educational Research Journal*, 7, 1, pp. 3–16.

DELAMONT, S. (1983) 'A woman's place in education: myths, monsters and misapprehensions', *Research Intelligence*, October, pp. 2–4.

EGGLESTON, J. (1979) 'The characteristics of educational research: mapping the domain', *British Educational Research Journal*, 5, 1, pp. 1–12.

EGGLESTON, J. and DELAMONT, S. (1983), *The Supervision of Students for Research Degrees with a Special Reference to Educational Studies*, BERA.

LAWTON, D. (1983) 'The politics of educational research', *Research Intelligence*, October, pp. 5–9.

McALEESE, R. and HAMILTON, D. (1978) *Understanding Classroom Life*, National Foundation for Educational Research.

NISBET, J. (1974) 'Educational research; the state of the art', *Proceedings of the Inaugural Meeting of the British Educational Research Association,* pp. 1–13.

SIMON, B. (1977) 'Educational research, which way?', *Research Intelligence,* Spring, pp. 2–7.

STENHOUSE, L. (1980) 'The study of samples and the study of cases', *British Educational Research Journal,* 6, 1, pp. 1–6.

STONES, E. (1975) 'The colour of conceptual learning', *Research Intelligence,* Winter, pp. 5–10.

VAUGHAN, J.E. (1983) *British Journals Concerning Education: A List for Research Workers and Others,* BERA.

WRAGG, E.C. (1982) 'From research into action', *British Educational Research Journal,* 8, 1, pp. 3–8.

WRIGLEY, J. (1976) 'Pitfalls in educational research', *Research Intelligence,* Autumn, pp. 2–4.

Bread and Dreams or Bread and Circuses? A Critique of 'Case Study' Research in Education

Paul Atkinson and Sara Delamont

> The 'SAFARI approach' . . . is less a methodology than a set of ethical principles translated as procedures for the design and conduct of research/evaluation projects. (Walker, 1981, p. 206)

> It was in (the SAFARI Project) that MacDonald and Walker, along with other colleagues, developed research designs which, for relatively low expenditure of resources, allowed a high degree of penetration normally associated with expensive and lengthy ethnographic studies. (Kushner, writing in *Bread and Dreams*, 1982, p. 258)

The two quotes from researchers based at CARE (Centre for Applied Research in Education, University of East Anglia) encapsulate the topics which we address in this paper.[1] Starting from the position of committed practitioners of interpretive research methods, particularly ethnography, in this paper we draw attention to three major problems in the methodology espoused by CARE, and its linked organizations in the USA and Australia. The paper is divided into three sections: an introductory part where the terms are defined; followed by sections on the inadequacies of methodology; the contradictions in invocations of 'evaluation', 'naturalism', and 'democracy' in research; and the interrelations of generalization, comparison and theorizing in case study. Planned educational change and curriculum innovation (*cf.* Stenhouse, 1975 and 1979) have become 'big business' and the evaluation of educational programmes has likewise been a growth area. With the development of this field of expertise and its professionalization, debate concerning appropriate research techniques and objectives has also grown. It is to this debate — or at least to one corner of it — that our paper is addressed. Our own research in this area (Howe and Delamont, 1973; Atkinson and Shone, 1982) was closest in style to a variety of educational evaluation variously known as 'illuminative', 'naturalistic', 'holistic', 'responsive' or 'case-study' research. On the other hand, there are many aspects of the way in which such research has been conducted and justified with which we take issue. There are certainly other approaches to educational research with which we are even less in sympathy, but commentary on those is beyond the scope of this paper. It is precisely because our own methodological commitments and perspectives are similar to those of the illuminative and case-study researchers that we can offer an informed critique of what remains a contentious area in educational research.

Defining Terms: Our and Theirs

Although an early and influential paper in the field referred to 'illuminative' evaluation (Parlett and Hamilton, 1972), in recent years the term 'case study' has gained much greater currency, and we shall use the latter term to cover the general area. For reasons which we shall discuss at greater length below, it is hard to provide any hard-and-fast definition of 'case study' and related approaches to educational evaluation. But there is a number of connotations, which represent the shared presuppositions and preoccupations of the network or invisible college of its practitioners. (The college is rendered visible in various edited collections of papers and conference proceedings, to which reference will be made: it is located in various institutional settings, of which CARE is the major British centre.)

In general terms, the approach denies the applicability of socalled 'scientific' methods of inquiry, as exemplified for instance in experimental or quasi-experimental research designs. It rests on the belief that the innovation to be examined cannot be treated simply as a set of objectives, or as a variable or variables to be measured. Innovations 'on paper' may be transformed radically, in the course of their actual implementation. The 'reality' to be investigated, then, is a complex social reality of everyday life in institutional settings. The emphasis is firmly — even exclusively — on 'process' rather than 'product' or outcomes (*cf.* Simons, 1981). Simons provides a helpful characterization of the style:

> Studies of the process of learning and schooling will tend to
> be descriptive/analytic, particular, small scale. They will
> record events in progress, document observations and draw
> on the judgments and perspectives of participants in the
> process — teachers, pupils, heads — in coming to understand
> observations and events in a specific context. Close descrip-
> tion both of practice and the social context is an important
> part of the study. Such descriptions provide opportunities for
> interpretations that elude other models of assessment or
> evaluation based on assumptions of comparability and eli-
> mination of variation. Such descriptions also provide oppor-
> tunities for more of the complexity of educational experience
> to be grasped and articulated. (Simons, 1981, p. 120)

The root metaphor of such a viewpoint is one of exploration and
discovery. Rather than investigating the 'official reality' of the promo-
ters of innovation, and confining attention to the stated objectives of
the innovation itself, case-study or illuminative evaluators pay full
attention to the unofficial and unforeseen aspects of the innovation
and its implementation. Those who advocate the use of 'behavioural
objectives' sometimes refer to them as necessary 'route-maps' to
direct the evaluator; the practitioners of case-study would be more
likely to point out that there always remains a good deal of uncharted
territory. The task of evaluators, then, may not be that of retracing a
predetermined route, but more akin to that of a 'search-party'.

It is remarkably difficult to provide anything approaching a
definitive account of case-study approaches to educational evaluation. There is undoubtedly a package of approaches to which
case-study workers would generally adhere, and we believe our
remarks above have provided a faithful — if brief and sketchy —
characterization of the main articles of faith. But close inspection of
the authors' statements reveals the elusiveness of the notion itself.

In the first place, it has proved extraordinarily difficult for the
practitioners themselves to furnish an adequate definition of their
own enterprise. Indeed, on the basis of their own pronouncements,
case-study evaluation would appear to be a 'paradigm' with none of
the requisites of a paradigm — agreed subject-matter, methods,
theories or exemplars. Given this, it is hardly surprising that such
definitions that do appear are quite extraordinarily imprecise. A
widely-quoted definition of case-study is that it is 'the study of an
instance in action', and 'the study of a bounded system' (*cf.* Adelman,
Jenkins and Kemmis, 1980). Such definitions (if they deserve the
term) seem to be of symbolic value to the research network of

devotees precisely insofar as they are vacuous and commit its members to remarkably little.

Confusion in this area is compounded when it is recognized that the unit of analysis ('case') can, in practice, mean just about anything:

> The case need not be a person or enterprise. It can be whatever 'bounded system' (to use Louis Smith's term) that is of interest. An institution, a program, a responsibility, a collection, or a population can be the case. (Stake, 1980, p. 64)

Stake goes on to protest that 'this is not to trivialize the notion of "case" . . . ', but it certainly does render it so general and vague as to be of next to no methodological value. Likewise, the notion of a 'bounded system' is unhelpful. Naturally occurring social 'systems' are not self-evidently 'bounded'. Their boundaries are matters of *construction*, by actors and analysts. What counts as a 'case' is therefore much more problematic than 'case-study' researchers seem to allow for. The same is true of the even more vague idea of 'an instance in action'. Cases and instances are recognizable only as cases or instances of something, and the range of potentially relevant dimensions or criteria is immense. It is therefore quite meaningless for authors of the case-study persuasion to write as if the world were populated by 'cases' whose status and existence were independent of methodological and theoretical concerns.

To some extent, the imprecision of which this is but an example is a reflection of the origins of the case-study movement. From the earliest formulations, such as that by Parlett and Hamilton (1972) 'illuminative evaluation' (as they called it) was portrayed as much in negative terms as its positive attributes. That is, the authors were as keen to establish what they were *not,* and to establish an oppositional heterodoxy as they were to provide a definitive account of their own position. This trend has continued in later publications emanating from the group, the members of which often characterize their work in terms of difference from other approaches to research. Parlett and Hamilton, for instance, distinguished their approach from the 'agri-cultural-botanical' paradigm, which they saw as the dominant model, based on the methods of field-experiments, psychometrics and the like. The movement has continued to identify itself in terms of oppositional and 'alternative' approaches, the proponents portraying themselves as renegade, heretical enfants terribles: on occasion they display the self-satisfaction of the heretical enthusiast.

Unfortunately, in the construction of this oppositional stance, the work of theoretical and methodological development has been neglected. In the early papers, appeals were made to traditions such as social anthropology as exemplars for the new paradigm. But as time has gone by, it has become apparent that for the most part case-study evaluators are content to invoke anthropology in a ritualized fashion. It has a totemic or fetishistic significance. But it is not apparent that the literature of case-study evaluation has been significantly affected by its authors' reading of British or American social/cultural anthropologists. (Some cultural anthropologists have become personally involved, and some individual authors, such as Louis Smith and Harry Wolcott must be exempt from this criticism.)

In short, precisely because of the failure of the researchers we are discussing to define their terms, we have difficulty in defining ours. Briefly we are criticizing a body of work which can be traced from the evaluation of the Humanities Curriculum Project and the Nuffield Resources for Learning Project, through UNCAL and SAFARI, to CARGO and *Bread and Dreams* (see Appendix and Walker, 1982 for details of these acronyms). Our criticisms apply to other projects conducted in the same general framework, notably Stake and Easley (1978) but we are concentrating on the work associated with MacDonald, Walker, Jenkins, Kushner, Norris and Stenhouse.

Our first area of criticism concerns methodology: or lack of it!

The Methodological Cop-Out

To some extent, the work of case-study practitioners has developed in parallel with more general scholarly interest in everyday life in schools and classrooms, and it draws eclectically on similar research methods. The methodology is likely to be based primarily on meaning-centred, qualitative data collection and analysis. Evaluation of this sort is not normally committed to any form of methodological purism (except in a negative sense, since some methods and research designs are ruled out). Rather, an eclectic approach is advocated, sometimes justified by appeal to between-method 'triangulation' (*cf.* Denzin, 1970; Webb *et al.*, 1966):

> In general, the techniques for collecting information for a case study are held in common with a wider tradition of sociological and anthropological fieldwork. Case study methodology is eclectic, although techniques and procedures in common use include observation (participant and non-participant),

interview (conducted with varying degrees of structure), audio-visual recording, field-note-taking, document collection, and the negotiation of products (for example discussing the accuracy of an account with those observed). (Adelman, Jenkins and Kemmis, 1980, pp. 48–49)

Appeal may also be made to the discovery of 'grounded theory' as advocated by Glaser and Strauss (1967) — see, for instance, Hamilton (1980, p. 81).

Case-study researchers protest that case-study methods are not thought of as a soft option. Hamilton (1980), for example, begins his paper by an explicit denial:

> Case study research is sometimes considered an immature science. It is claimed, for instance, that as an apparently non-technical mode of inquiry it is a suitable 'shallow end' activity for the statistically naive newcomer to educational research.

> This paper challenges such a viewpoint . . . (Hamilton, 1980, p. 78)

Nonetheless, such a message would appear to be implicit in the programmatic statements of many of the authors. Methodological sophistication is not a marked characteristic of the genre. Indeed, methodological and theoretical expertise may even be denied explicitly by particular advocates of the approach, as in Walker's (1981) remark with which we opened the paper.

As we have indicated, the methodological commitments are often adumbrated in a negative sense: the title of one collection of papers, *Beyond the Numbers Game* (Hamilton *et al.*, [Eds.] 1977) captures this nicely. This negativity leaves little room for positive commitments: for instance:

> Case studies should not be equated with observational studies, participant or otherwise . . .

> Case studies are not simply pre-experimental . . .

> 'Case study' is not the name for a standard methodological package . . . (Adelman, Jenkins and Kemmis, 1980, p. 48)

On the other hand, it is true to say that in practice a recognizable methodological commitment is discernible, which corresponds fairly well to that connoted by the *ethnographic* approach. In the context of educational research generally, ethnographic research is a relatively new phenomenon, and has enjoyed something of a boom (*cf.* Delamont, 1984), although it is now a good deal less innovative than it was when Parlett and Hamilton first published their account. But in advocating a (vaguely) ethnographic approach, the case-study writers often seem in danger of reinventing the wheel: what is worse, they seem rather slapdash wheelwrights at that.

The published accounts betray alarmingly little acquaintance with the fact that qualitative and documentary methods have been in use by sociologists and anthropologists for many years, and — more significantly — that there has been a great deal of reflection and writing on the methodology of research of this sort. Shipman (1981) has drawn attention to such shortcomings in the pages of what he calls 'parvenu evaluation'. He points out that 'the curriculum is but one subject for study through established research methods' (p. 111), and the claim for bespoke, supposedly innovative methods in fact merely leads to the neglect of existing 'mainstream' research methods literature:

> Illuminative evaluation often seems ... innocent of fifty years of debate within social science. Malinowski detailed the pros and cons of participant observation in 1922, a year after Anderson published his observational study of hobos in Chicago. The Chicago school was particularly active in using such methods and Thrasher published the first detailed account of the approach in 1928, based on a decade of work in the field. Discussing evaluation within education can be depressing because of the divorce from this long tradition within social science. It is possible to lecture and research in curriculum evaluation without realising that the tradition is there for us. (Shipman, 1981, p. 113)

In a similar vein, Spindler has written of the dangers inherent in the sudden fashion for ethnographic research in educational settings:

> To those of us who have long struggled to persuade educators that ethnographic studies would help illuminate the educational process and fellow scientists that they should undertake ethnographic studies of this process, the sudden wave of popularity is exhilarating. It is also alarming. Inevitably, any movement that rapidly acquires many followers has some of the qualities of a fad, and this is true of educational ethnography. It is not surprising that some work called 'ethnography' is marked by obscurity of purpose, lax relationships between

concepts and observation, indifferent or absent conceptual structure and theory, weak implementation of research method, confusion about whether there should be hypotheses and, if so, how they should be tested, confusion about whether quantitative methods can be relevant, unrealistic expectations about the virtues of 'ethnographic' evaluation, and so forth. (Spindler, 1982, pp. 1–2)

The dangers and pitfalls of which Spindler writes are all too obviously present in the conduct and reporting of case-study evaluation.

In *Bread and Dreams*, for example, Kushner (1983, p. 258) claims that: 'A combination of issues focusing intensive interviewing, selective observation and the negotiation of accounts with participants made it possible to complete a school case-study on a base of seven days fieldwork'. The reader wishing to pursue this extravagant claim is referred to Simons (1980): 'the definitive collection of writings'. Simons (1980) contains little in the way of methodological discussion or reflexivity. It is our contention that the case study research tradition is seriously deficient due to both inadequate methods and a lack of methodological self-awareness.

The methodological self-awareness we are referring to here would not imply a radical doubt over the essential purpose and value of ethnographic work. On the contrary, it would recognize its value and importance even more. It would treat the methods seriously, rather than adopting the essentially philistine attitude that 'anyone can do it'. This introduces our next concern, the related issues of research, evaluation, 'democracy', and naturalism.

Research, Evaluation, Democracy and Naturalism

We have called the case-study workers anti-intellectual and objected to their lack of scholarship. This attitude may be justified, as in MacDonald (1974) by the insistence on a basic difference between 'research' and 'evaluation'. Thus the professional evaluator may simultaneously be invested with special insight and experience on the one hand, and absolved from the theoretical and methodological constraints of the 'researcher'. The distinction is spurious. MacDonald bases his account on a crudely stereotyped distinction between the 'pure' academic and the applied evaluator. He quite absurdly, for instance, claims that academic researchers are insensitive to the social and political context of their research, in contrast to 'evaluators'. This is the product of a rhetoric of self-justification and congratulation on MacDonald's part, rather than a reflection of research practice. No social or educational research is 'pure' in that sense; nor can 'applied' research escape the requirements of rigour and critical reflection.

It is true that this anti-intellectual or anti-academic tenor to such evaluation does, in various quarters, reflect a deliberate commitment on the part of the researchers. For some research workers, the task of evaluation is essentially a collaborative one, in which the evaluators and the practitioners (for example, the teachers) work together in generating shared perspectives, in reorganizing and accounting for the problems they encounter and so on. Thought of from this point of view the research process may be classed as a 'democratic' exercise. At the same time it may be suggested that a concern for 'theory' or 'methods' should be deprecated: it is seen as an essentially mystificatory exercise, in which 'experts' parade their superiority over practitioners. Expertise is seen as divisive, in contrast to the democratic ideal of collaborative partnership.

Walker, one of the leading representatives of the CARE tradition, is explicit about the 'democratic' implications of his own commitment to 'naturalistic' research. The research begins and ends within the everyday, 'natural attitude' of teachers, pupils and other participants:

> First it assumes that the research will start from the natural language of description of 'natural' observers and attempt to remain as close to them as possible. This is to say much more than that the researcher must simply avoid jargon and attempt to write lucidly ...

> Second, it assumes that research will remain as close as possible to the organizational constraints facing 'natural' observers ...

> Third, it assumes research will remain as close as possible to the kinds of resources normally available to 'natural' observers. (Walker, 1974, pp. 25–26)

The 'natural' observers Walker has in mind here would be teachers, pupils, teacher educators and advisors and inspectors. They all have practical interests and skills in observing, participating in and understanding classroom life.

There is thus an emphasis upon research as an essentially vernacular or demotic undertaking. Now it is perfectly true that ethnographic research explicitly rests upon the homology between everyday life and the methods used to study it. But that is not tantamount to an identity between the practical concerns of social actors and the theoretical concerns of sociological or anthropological analysis. Walker maintains that case-study work 'would start with, and remain close to, the commonsense knowledge of the practitioner . . . ' In itself, that aim is hardly contentious. All ethnography must concern itself with subjects' common sense. But that is not in itself an argument for undertaking commonsense investigations. Quite the reverse: the successful unravelling and explication of mundane beliefs and actions demand the suspension of common sense, not its uncritical endorsement.

It is worth noting in passing that Walker's appeal to 'natural' observers contains some special pleading. He constructs the 'natural' observer as a sort of primitive innocent, whose natural state corresponds remarkably with Walker's preferred approach to research. For instance, part of the section referred to above continues in the following way:

> . . . it assumes research will remain as close as possible to the kinds of resources normally available to 'natural' observers. Incidentally, this may not imply 'simplicity' of technique since many practitioners can now obtain access to video-taped cctv but may find even small scale testing or survey programmes beyond their scope. (*ibid.*, p. 26)

There seems absolutely no reason to suppose (a) that, say, small-scale survey research is actually beyond the resources of practitioners, or that the administration of tests is not feasible for them: many in-service B.Ed. and M.Ed. dissertations attest to the contrary; (b) that the use and understanding of such techniques is beyond their commonsense understanding, even if they do not actually use them. We see no reason to suppose that a grasp of elementary research techniques of a 'traditional' sort is beyond the ken of all those involved in educational practice.

While Walker's pronouncements are intended to be 'democratic' in their effect, we believe their implications to be very different. It is intended to demystify the activities of research workers, to eliminate the sense of an elite and remote cadre of evaluation experts. MacDonald (for example, 1974) has also promoted a view of 'democratic' evaluation, contrasting it with what he refers to as 'bureaucratic' and 'autocratic' modes respectively. His stance derives from an explicitly political and ethical commitment to 'an informed citizenry': 'the evaluator acts as a broker in exchanges of information between groups who want knowledge of each other' (1974, p. 15). As he himself puts it, 'The key justificatory concept is "the right to know"' (p. 18).

Smith *et al* (1981) have produced a typology of approaches to evaluation, based on MacDonald's position, and that of Lindblom and Cohen (1979), including the 'client/democratic' stance, which they characterize in this way:

> . . . the subjects or participants in the study have final control over entry, definition of problems, procedures, ownership, and release of data and interpretations, and so forth. They are the audience of the exercise. The negotiation process between the researcher/evaluator and the multiple individuals and subgroups involved in the program or activity is escalated in importance, focus, and time involvement. In an important sense, MacDonald is advocating political change in liberal, democratic, national states by exposing gaps between the realities of educational settings and the idealism most of us profess in our ideologies. (p. 86)

It is evident, therefore, that contemporary case-study evaluation rests on two closely related presuppositions — appealing to a demotic naturalism and a democratic ethic. 'Naturalism' is invoked explicitly in numerous papers (for example, Kushner and Norris, 1980–81; Kemmis, 1980). Barton and Lawn (1980–81) have argued that the CARE version of 'naturalistic' inquiry and reportage is best understood as heir to the tradition of documentary social observation of which Mass Observation was a particularly pertinent exemplar. This tradition is an important one in British social thought, and the strengths of the CARE case study approach are its strengths. But the weaknesses are shared too. As Barton and Lawn argue, the commitment to naturalism does not remove problems of interpretation and theory, but can serve to mask them:

> We would also argue that if assumptions are not made explicit — that is, about the nature of society and the reflexive role of the individual — then the 'outsider', who may be a reader or researcher, is not encouraged to analyse critically or refute the view offered. It is offered as natural not evaluative. (p. 21)

Case-study researchers explicitly draw upon models from naturalistic writing, including works of fiction, and may illustrate their own accounts with fictional accounts (*cf.* Walker, 1981). The critic will wish to point out that the most 'naturalistic' or 'realistic' literary account is the outcome of highly artful and conventional effort on the part of its maker. It is itself theory-laden:

> Naturalism in the novel, especially the novels of the late nineteenth century French school, used finely drawn individual characters, their real life settings and dialogue, to illustrate a thesis that was fashionable at the time — social Darwinism. The very fact that this thesis was part of the social norms of its audience probably made the novels 'feel' more naturalistic — they expected the situations to be like that. In retrospect, the detail and the observation seem at the mercy of the implicit thesis. (Barton and Lawn, 1980–81, p. 21)

Case-study evaluators are by no means alone in promoting a 'naturalistic' style with insufficient attention to its own conventional character (*cf.* Atkinson, 1982). Those who are responsible for the production of written accounts certainly should be aware of the nature of description and narration, as Walker (1981) advocates. But that is not an argument for substituting literary style for theory or method. And while the practitioners may reject epistemological orthodoxy or uniformity, there is a remarkable uniformity of style to their products. Rather than the straightforward, vernacular craft it is often claimed, case-study is a highly artful enterprise.

While we recognize the attractions in the 'democratic' argument, we dissent from the implications drawn from it. A denial of theory and method is, we believe, a denial of responsibility — of responsibility for one's research activities and conclusions. It suggests the paradox of a group of 'experts' in evaluation, part of whose stock in trade consists of a denial of expertise. It is clear, however, that they do have 'expertise': they do operate with distinctive methods and assumptions and the studies they undertake have clearly recognizable characteristics. A refusal to treat seriously issues of methods is, we repeat, a denial of responsibility rather than a tenable position on the matter of evaluation.

It should be clear that we believe that in the context of case-study research a concern for ethics too often supplants equally important issues of theory and method. It is not our intention in the rest of this paper to attempt to remedy all the conceptual shortcomings of this self-proclaimed 'paradigm'. We shall concentrate on a restricted number of muddles. These are all concerned with the nature of the 'particular' and the 'general'. Here the character of case-study research is clearly exemplified, and the confusions reveal some of the methodological limits of the approach.

Paul Atkinson and Sara Delamont

Generalization, Comparison and Theorizing

Our final themes are those of generalizing, comparing and theorizing. The proponents of case-study research often distinguish their enterprise from other research styles and approaches through a stress upon the unique, the particular, the 'instance'. The title of one of the edited collections encapsulates this: *The Science of the Singular* (Simons, [Ed.] 1980). We wish to argue that in their approach to 'cases', the authors are profoundly mistaken.

The paper by Hamilton (1980), from which the 'science of the singular' aphorism derives, represents a relatively sophisticated and well-informed defence of the case-study position. It is, however, flawed. Like too many statements deriving from this research network, it rests too glibly on crude stereotypes of research traditions: strangely — in the light of the apparent rejection of methodological orthodoxy — it insists on an extreme version of qualitative research and a thoroughgoing rejection of alternative approaches. The characterization of qualitative, ethnographic research is so extreme as to deviate from positions adhered to by most sociologists and anthropologists (though their disciplines are invoked).

Hamilton rests his argument on a series of contrasts between case-study and survey — proposing the latter as essentially positivist. Although it is not possible to rehearse all the counter-arguments here, it must be objected that the supposed opposition between 'naturalism' and 'positivism' is inadequate (*cf.* Hammersley and Atkinson, 1983), as is the assumption that survey research is to be equated with positivist assumptions (*cf.* Marsh, 1982).

The most contentious of Hamilton's distinctions concerns the nature of generalization and interpretation. It is claimed that survey research is concerned with generalization, and further, that this concern reflects a belief in the 'uniformity of nature'. Astonishingly, Hamilton maintains that survey researchers are so committed to such a belief that 'By this procedural logic (of the relation of a sample to a population) it is then quite acceptable to extrapolate from Scottish samples to US samples, from nineteenth century data to contemporary results, and so on' (Hamilton, 1980, p. 86). While sloppy reasoning of this sort no doubt takes place, we know of nothing in any formulation of 'positivist' social research remotely suggesting its legitimacy.

By the same token, it is suggested that 'generalization' is *not* a concern for the qualitative studies of particular institutions. The emphasis is all upon the unique characteristics of each, idiosyncratic 'case'. Referring to recent ethnographies of schools, Hamilton claims 'They treat each case as empirically distinct and, in contrast to survey analysis, do not automatically presume that different instances can be thrown together to form a homogeneous aggregate' (p. 79). Survey research does not 'automatically assume' that either, of course, and certainly does not 'throw together' instances in the insouciant way that phrase implies. On the other hand, qualitative research *does* aggregate 'instances'. Data are regularly collected into typologies, and at least an ordinal level of measurement is regularly invoked by fieldworkers in the claim that, say, things happen more or less frequently, are of more or less importance, are more or less disruptive and so on.

Likewise, it is simply not true that the traditions of qualitative research from which case-study research draws inspiration eschews generalization. We are certainly not dealing only with a series of self-contained, one off studies which bear no systematic relationship to each other. The studies of social anthropologists, for instance, have consistently reflected the shared theories and methods of major schools and movements (such as structural-functionalism or culture-and-personality theory). The accumulated literature of anthropology represents the massively successful working-out of a number of related, evolving 'paradigms'. Anthropologists do document the particularities of given cultures and communities; but they do much more than that. The same can be said of relevant traditions in sociology, such as symbolic interactionism.

In fact, the development of ethnographic work in sociology and anthropology rests on a principle of *comparative* analysis. If studies are not explicitly developed into more general frameworks, then they will be doomed to remain isolated one-off affairs, with no sense of cumulative knowledge or developing theoretical insight. Regrettably, this failing of 'illuminators' renders their work a rather pale version of qualitative research. This is particularly noticeable in the extent to which their focus remains fixed on the particular research setting, with little attention to other educational settings, and practically none to social settings of other sorts. They neglect the insights which may be gained from similar ethnographic work in such institutions as hospitals, prisons, hostels, therapeutic communities, old peoples' homes and so on. Yet all these settings — as well as many others — exhibit the same general processes as the evaluator may wish to understand in an educational programme: they too may be marked by inter-professional conflict, by tension between staff and inmates, by competing definitions of the institutional goals, by upheavals consequent upon planned innovations and so on. If one is to adopt an essentially ethnographic approach to research, then the work will remain inadequate unless such comparative perspectives are employed (Delamont, 1981; Wolcott, 1981).

This point concerning comparative perspectives relates directly to the issue of the generalizability of such research and its 'findings'. The analytic approach to such studies should be conceived of in terms of *formal* concepts — or, as Lofland (1971) calls them, *generic* problems. These formal concepts are abstract, ideal-typical, notions which characterize features, problems and issues which may be common to a range of different concrete settings. A well known example of this sort of concept is Goffman's (1968) formulation of the 'total institution' which he uses to portray features which are common to a wide variety of apparently diverse organizations (mental hospitals, monasteries, military camps, etc.). Thus Goffman's primary analysis of the mental hospital is developed through explicit and implicit comparison with these other institutions, which are shown, in *formal* terms, to have common features.

The development of such formal concepts thus frees the researcher from the potential strait-jacket of restricting attention only to the particular setting directly available to study. Indeed, the emphasis is, if anything, reversed. Ethnographers in sociology have sometimes been taxed with the charge of devoting too much attention to 'trivial', 'exotic' or 'bizarre' settings of everyday life, but these settings are used to illustrate and display the *formal* properties of social life. As Rock (1979) puts it:

> The career of the high school teacher, the organization of a ward for tuberculosis patients, the moral history of the taxi-dancer, the career of a mental patient, and transactions between police and juvenile delinquents present materials for the dissection of elementary social forms. They are explored to illuminate a simple grammar of sociation, a grammar whose rules give order to the allocation of territorial rights, the programming of timetables, and the meeting of diverse groups. More important, it is a grammar which is intended to provide recipes for an understanding of the abstract properties of social life.

It is the case, we recognize, that evaluators are not primarily in the business of generating sociological or social psychological theory as such. Walker (1982, p. 200) says there is 'a general consensus amongst those in the field that even if theoretical progress is possible or desirable (both points being at issue), it will only emerge gradually as a residual accumulation ... ' But theory in this context is not a self-contained, de-contextualized activity. While the formal concepts are derived from concrete instances and settings, they are only recognizable, and are only realized in their concrete manifestations. There is a constant interplay between 'theory', 'method' and 'findings'. At the same time, if evaluators are unwilling to grapple with the formal concepts and theories, then their work is doomed to be little more than a series of one-off, self-contained reports, all of which return to 'square one', conceptually speaking.

Theory cannot be left to accumulate, any more than the issue of generalization can be avoided. Yet here, too, we find the writings of the case-study exponents confused.

Robert Stake (1980) has attempted to come to terms with the issue of generalization. His approach to the problem serves, we argue, further to highlight the weaknesses of a commitment to naturalistic case-study inquiry, as currently proposed. Stake's key concept is 'naturalistic generalization':

> What becomes useful understanding is a full and thorough knowledge of the particular, recognizing it also in new and foreign contexts.

> That knowledge is a form of generalization too, not scientific induction but *naturalistic generalization,* arrived at by recognizing the similarities of objects and issues in and out of context and by sensing the natural covariations of happenings. To generalize this way is to be both intuitive and empirical, and not idiotic. (Stake, 1980, pp. 68–69)

In some ways such a formulation seems similar to our own emphasis upon the importance of generic analytic categories. The stumbling block is that Stake repeatedly insists on the tacit, the experiential and the private. Likewise he repeatedly contrasts such notions with the 'scientific', 'propositional formulations' and the like. Again, his views parallel the well-worn distinction between 'science' or 'positivism' and 'naturalism'.

Stake suggests that what he calls naturalistic generalizations will be of more value to the users or consumers of research. He invokes Howard Becker:

> Sociologist Howard Becker spoke of an irreducible conflict between sociological perspective and the perspective of everyday life. Which is superior? It depends on the circumstance of

course. For publishing in the sociological journals, the scientific perspective is better; but for reporting to lay audiences and for studying lay problems, the lay perspective will often be superior.

In these formulations, Stake confuses a number of issues. The way in which a study is *reported* (for example, to a 'lay' audience) should not be mistaken for a methodological principle in deriving and warranting knowledge. Likewise, tacit knowledge pervades all reasoning in the natural and social sciences. But that is no excuse for the failure to develop explicit formal analysis, as Stake advocates.

Furthermore, the appeal to 'naturalistic generalization' seems to pass on to the consumers of research the right and capacity to define what is to count as knowledge. This is comfortable for a Stake if the hypothetical user can be constructed in such a way as to want and to appreciate 'naturalistic' inquiry, 'vicarious experience' and the like. As with MacDonald's 'democratic' ideal, it translates into research practice provided researcher and other participants operate within a morally consensual framework, or the researcher can impose his or her definition of what counts as evaluation.

Concluding Remarks

The criticisms we make here are not new nor unique (Parsons, 1976; Shipman, 1981). We raised these issues with Parlett and Hamilton (1972) twelve years ago, and have debated them with people from CARE since. In 1978 one of us wrote:

> Paradoxically, the relative shortcomings of the 'illuminative' approach mean that its proponents are, in the last analysis, as limited as the practitioners of the denigrated 'agricultural-botany'. Without an adequately formulated body of theory or methods, the illuminators have been, and will be, unable to progress and generate a coherent, cumulative research tradition. They cannot transcend the short-term practicalities of any given programme of curriculum innovation. They merely substitute one variety of atheoretical 'findings' — based mainly on observation and interview — for another — based mainly on test scores. (Delamont, 1978)

We see no reason to dissent from that verdict here.

Notes

1 The arguments in this paper have been discussed with a variety of colleagues since 1970. We have debated them with Clem Adelman, Len Barton, David Hamilton, Barry MacDonald, Malcolm Parlett, Bob Stake and Rob Walker and the late Lawrence Stenhouse in print and face to face. We gave versions of this paper at the 1981 conference of the SfAA in Edinburgh and the 1982 BERA conference at St. Andrews, and received useful feedback. We have both conducted evaluations of educational innovations (Howe and Delamont, 1973; Atkinson and Shone, 1982), and conducted fieldwork in educational institutions.

We are grateful to Mrs Mytle Robins for typing this version of our paper.

References

ADELMAN, C., KEMMIS, S. and JENKINS, D. (1980) 'Rethinking case study: notes from the second Cambridge conference', in SIMONS, H. (Ed.) — see below.

ATKINSON, P. (1979) *Research Design in Ethnographic Research*, Course DE304, Block 3, Unit 5, Milton Keynes, The Open University.

ATKINSON, P. (1982) 'Writing ethnography', in HELLE, H.J. (Ed.) *Kultur und Institution*, Berlin, Dunker and Humblot.

ATKINSON, P. and SHONE, D. (1982) *Everyday Life in Two Industrial Training Units*, Köln, IFAPLAN.

BARTON, L. and LAWN, M. (1980/81) 'Back inside the whale' and 'Recording the natural world', *Interchange*, 3, 4, pp. 2–26.

DELAMONT, S. (1978) 'Sociology and the classroom', in BARTON, L. and MEIGHAN, R. (Eds.) *Sociological Interpretations of Schools and Classrooms*, Driffield, Yorks, Nafferton Books.

DELAMONT, S. (1981) 'All too familiar?', *Educational Analysis*, 3, 1, pp. 69–84.

DELAMONT, S. (Ed.) (1984) *Readings in Classroom Interaction*, London, Methuen.

DENZIN, N. (1970) *The Research Act*, Chicago, Aldine.

GOFFMAN, E. (1968) *Asylums*, Harmondsworth, Penguin.

GOFFMAN, E. (1971) *The Presentation of Self in Everyday Life*, Harmondsworth, Penguin.

HAMILTON, D. (1980) 'Some contrasting assumptions about case study research and survey analysis', in SIMONS, H. (Ed.) — see below.

HAMILTON, D. et al. (Eds.) (1977) *Beyond the Numbers Game*, London, Macmillan.

HAMMERSLEY, M. and ATKINSON, P. (1983) *Ethnography: Principles in Practice*, London, Tavistock.

HOWE, J.A.M. and DELAMONT, S. (1973) 'Pupils' answer to computer language', *Education in the North*, 10, pp. 73–78.

KEMMIS, S. (1980) 'The imagination of the case and the invention of the study', in SIMONS, H. (Ed.) — see below.

KLAPP, O. (1958) 'Social types', *American Sociological Review*, 23, pp. 674–680.

KUSHNER, S. (1982) 'The research process', MacDONALD, B. *et al.* (Eds.) *Bread and Dreams*, Norwich, CARE.

KUSHNER, S. and NORRIS, D. (1980–81) 'Interpretation, negotiation and validity in naturalistic research', *Interchange*, 11, 4, pp. 26–36.

LINDBLOM, C. and COHEN, D. (1979) *Usable Knowledge*, New Haven, Conn., Yale U.P.

LOFLAND, J. (1971) *Analysing Social Settings*, Belmont, California, Wadsworth.

MARSH, C. (1982) *Survey Research*, London, Allen and Unwin.

PARLETT, M. and HAMILTON, D. (1972) *Evaluation as Illumination*. Occasional paper No. 9, Centre for Educational Research in the Educational Sciences, University of Edinburgh. Reprinted in HAMILTON, D. *et al.* (1977) — see above.

PARSONS, C. (1981) 'A policy for educational evaluation', in LACEY, C. and LAWTON, D. (Eds.) *Issues in Evaluation and Accountability*, London, Methuen.

RAWLINGS, B. (1980) 'The production of facts in a therapeutic community', ATKINSON, P. and HEATH, C. (Eds.) *Medical Work: Realities and Routines*, Farnborough, Gower.

ROCK, P. (1979) *The Making of Symbolic Interactionism*, London, Macmillan.

SHIPMAN, M. (1981) 'Parvenu evaluation', in SMETHERHAM, D. (Ed.) *Practising Evaluation*, Driffield, Yorks, Nafferton Books.

SIMONS, H. (Ed.) (1980) *Towards a Science of the Singular*, Norwich, CARE.

SIMONS, H. (1981) 'Process evaluation in schools', LACEY, C. and LAWTON, D. (Eds.) *Issues in Evaluation and Accountability*, London, Methuen.

SMITH, L.M. *et al.* (1981) 'Observer role and field study knowledge', *Educational Evaluation and Policy Analysis*, 3, 3, pp. 83–90.

SPINDLER, G. (1982) 'General Introduction', in SPINDLER, G. (Ed.) *Doing the Ethnography of Schooling*, New York, Holt.

STAKE, R. and EASLEY, J. (Eds.) (1978) *Case Studies in Science Education*, University of Illinois, Urbana-Champaigne, CIRCE.

STAKE, R. (1980) 'The case study method in social inquiry', SIMONS, H. (Ed.) — see above.

STENHOUSE, L. (1975) *An Introduction to Curriculum Research and Development*, London, Heinemann.

STENHOUSE, L. (1979) *Curriculum Research and Development in Action*, London, Heinemann.

WALKER, R. (1974) 'Classroom research: a view from Safari', MacDONALD, B. and WALKER, R. (Eds.) *Innovation, Evaluation Research and the Problem of Control*, Norwich, CARE.

WALKER, R. (1981) 'Getting involved in curriculum research: a personal history', in LAWN, M. and BARTON, L. (Eds.) *Rethinking Curriculum Studies*, London, Croom Helm.

WALKER, R. (1982) 'The use of case studies in applied research and evaluation', in HARTNETT, A. (Ed.) *The Social Sciences in Educational Studies,* London, Heinemann.

WEBB, E. *et al.* (1966) *Unobtrusive Measures,* Chicago, Rand McNally.

WOLCOTT, H.F. (1977) *Teachers versus Technocrats,* Centre for Educational Policy and Management, Eugene, Oregon, University of Oregon.

WOLCOTT, H.F. (1981) 'Confessions of a "trained" observer', POPKEWITZ, T.S. and TABACHNICK, B.R. (Eds.) *The Study of Schooling,* New York, Praeger.

Appendix

One difficulty for 'outsiders' working on the products of the case-study researchers is the scattered, fragmentary and unpublished source material. We have listed below mimeoed, lithoed and other 'semi-published' materials which we have read in order to produce this paper.

The output of CARE, University of East Anglia, is available from CARE by mail order.

ADELMAN, C. and GIBBS, I. (1979) *A Study of Student Choice in the Context of Institutional Change,* Report to the DES.

ELLIOTT, J. and MACDONALD, B. (Eds.) (1975) *People in Classrooms,* Norwich, CARE.

JENKINS, D. *et al.* (1979) *Chocolate, Cream, Soldiers,* Coleraine, New University of Ulster.

MACDONALD, B. and WALKER, R. (Eds.) (1974) *Innovation, Evaluation Research and the Problem of Control: Safari Papers 1,* Norwich, CARE.

MACDONALD, B. *et al.* (1975) *The Programme at Two,* Norwich, CARE.

MACDONALD, B. (Ed) (1978) *The Experience of Innovation,* Norwich, CARE.

MACDONALD, B. *et al.* (1981) *Evaluators at Work,* Köln, IFAPLAN.

MACDONALD, B. *et al.* (1982) *Bread and Dreams,* Norwich, CARE.

NORRIS, N. (Ed.) (1977) *Theory in Practice: Safari Papers Two,* Norwich, CARE.

SIMONS, H. (Ed.) (1980) *Towards a Science of the Singular,* Norwich, CARE.

STAKE, R. and EASLEY, J. (Eds.) (1978) *Case Studies in Science Education,* University of Illinois at Urbana-Champaigne, CIRCE.

WALKER, R. (1981) *The Observational Work of Local Authority Inspectors and Advisors,* Norwich, CARE.

WOLCOTT, H.F. (1977) *Teachers Versus Technocrats,* Eugene, Oregon, Centre for Education Policy and Management.

The reader may also wish to consult *Interchange,* Vol. 11, No. 4, 1980–81, a special issue on 'The social observation tradition in British educational research'.

The Assumptions of Educational Research: The Last Twenty Years in Great Britain

Clem Adelman and Michael F.D. Young

The history of educational research in the USA is available as a primer in the form of Cronbach and Suppes' book (1969). Through that book current lines of research in the USA can be traced to earlier endeavours, with the caveat that the social, economic and political contexts which contribute to the significance of the topics of research have altered over the past century. A comparable history of educational research in Great Britain has yet to be written. It is our understanding that the development of research in Great Britain has had many parallels to the USA; child study and questionnaire preceded mental testing and child development. Relationships between intelligence and size of family, social class and other variables, became the dominant field of enquiry for educational research from the 1920s to the 1950s. An experimental variety of psychology dominated, and still dominates, educational research today in spite of at least twenty years of cogent critique. Many of the so-called 'new' approaches to educational research in Great Britain — case study, classroom interaction, anthropological (minuscule compared to the tradition in the USA) and symbolic interactionist — can be traced back to at least as far as 1900, although educational research based on phenomonological premises or Marxist analysis, was not conducted until the 1960s.

In this article we consider assumptions from two different approaches to educational research and give some examples of the extent to which research has influenced policy. We bring a historical perspective into our discussion because we have found that the contrasting assumptions that we are about to suggest, in spite of changes in language, methodology and social context, are in continuity with readily recognizable perspectives in the past. The two broad categories across which we will make contrasts we will call the empiricist and the interpretive.

The empiricist tradition assumes that knowledge of educational practice can be collected through the senses, assisted, in many cases, by instrumentation. Linked to the empiricist view on what is to be counted as data, is the positivists' view on how theory should be constructed. The positivist believes that by collecting sufficient pieces of appropriate information, a picture would begin to emerge from the particulars and furthermore that someone will realize the general principles or laws on which the particulars can be organized. That empiricist, positivistic view of research is based upon the nineteenth century successes of the physical sciences, a method that physicists themselves have become increasingly sceptical about. 'No experiment ever proved a theory' was a principle source of angst to the audiences of science schoolteachers at the recent history and philosophy of science lectures of Professor Post at the Centre for Science Education, Chelsea College, London.

Empiricist research in education (and the social sciences) assumes the observer's version of events to be superior in reliability and validity to that of the actors (or subjects of study); the observer's version is the only reliable account with claims to objectivity which can be used as the basis of constructing theory. This exclusivity of observer's account, otherwise known as the etic approach (Pike, 1967), seeks prediction as a scientific goal and 'rigor' through forms of measurement and quantification amenable to mathematical and statistical analysis. Very often the research sets out to test hypotheses which are in themselves derived from a theory, itself in various stages of development. Notably this form of research tends to ignore its own interaction with the social world that it is studying and takes a normative perspective on practice, on institutions, on rules and sanctions and inevitably lacks any explicit sense of historical perspective.

It is apparent in recent research in this tradition that there is considerable ambiguity in relation to policy and politics. For instance, one of the issues in the so-called 'great debate' on education which followed Callaghan's Ruskin College speech was the appropriateness and effectiveness of 'formal' as against 'informal' methods of teaching. That issue had already been explored, for instance by research in association with the Plowden Report and the work of Resnick (1972), Barnes (1969) and Walker and Adelman (1972, 1976).

These studies when conducted raised limited interest amongst curriculum developers, English teachers and some educational researchers. At that time 'child centred' education was assumed to have been accepted and widely practised even in secondary schools. Those researches were seen as interesting enquiries, interchanges in educational practice that had already been widely affirmed.

By the late 1970s in a changed political climate, 'informal versus formal' teaching had become embroiled in a wide debate about educational standards and accountability — a point that no educational researcher could ignore. *Teaching Styles and Pupil Progress* (Bennett, 1976), for all its adverse reviews indicating inadequate design, lack of internal reliability (a cornerstone of empirical research), statistical misapplications and yawning questions of interpretation, appeared at a historically critical moment. It was the right time and the right place, the right issue affecting public opinion, the DES and government policy on curriculum and teaching. Like the good empiricist positivist only seeking 'truths' within the confines of pre-specified variables, the main author, Bennett, during a BBC television programme about the research said, with some verisimilitude, that he had no idea that his research was going to be used as key evidence in the ideological attack upon informal, child-centred, teaching.

Research of the interpretive type takes actors' (research subjects') accounts as valid as descriptions and for constructing categories of action within a particular culture (be it at home or school). Set alongside observers' accounts, the realities of the actors' accounts provide the basis for a rich description of practice and events. Often discrepancies between actors' accounts (emic) and between emic and etic accounts become manifest in the course of analysis. These discrepancies are pursued by further research often through the interview but also by observation, participant observation, diaries and reactions to observers' draft reports.[1]

In the interpretive tradition the pursuit of discrepancy *between* actors' accounts is as important as that of the discrepancy within observers' accounts. The actor's right of access to other actors' accounts used in research reports becomes itself a practical issue in interpretive research. By contrast, in empiricist research such involvement of actors in validating researchers' accounts is restricted and undesirable and often termed, from the experimental paradigm, contamination.

Pursuit of discrepancies between actors' accounts also raises the practical issue of actors' right to confidentiality and of their right to anonymity in reports that are to be published. Empiricist research assumes that anonymity is achieved through presentation of reports in quantified form. Indeed, the Rutter research took anonymity to such an extreme that the presentation of data as displayed in the book precludes attempts to piece together the related information about each school (Rutter, 1979). To the reader no links can be made between the variables to build up a picture of each school.

Interpretive research builds its data on and around the particular instance by a process of constant comparison (Glaser, 1964) or analytic induction (Robinson, 1969) or progressive focusing (Parlett and Hamilton, 1972). This process was devised by American sociologists such as Cooley, Zaniecki, Park and Burgess during the early part of this century.

Few educational researchers working in the interpretive paradigm would go as far as the anthropologists Levi-Strauss (1968) and Needham (1976) in arguing that only the actors' accounts are valid for the purposes of analysis and theory construction; Torode's (1976) work is nearest to that position amongst British educational researchers. In the pursuit of discrepancy between and within actors' and observers' accounts, researchers working in the interpretive paradigm compare, alternately, the etic and the emic accounts. Such methodology is exemplified by the case study (MacDonald and Walker, 1975; Walker, 1974; Simons, 1980), where a key criterion of adequacy is that discrepancies are pursued and the derivation of categorical relationships and the relationship between 'variables' are explicit and exhaustive.

Walker (1983) on the basis of his experience as a case study worker (for example, 1978, 1982), provides what amounts to warning signals to those embarking on educational research using case study methodology. Walker writes about the difficulty of maintaining a suspension of judgment, avoiding co-option, of the difficulties of dealing with informants' reactions to case study drafts given the informants' agreed right of access and comment on those drafts, relying too heavily on the single source of data at the interview and the problems raised by intervention in the lives of others through this form of research. These are over and above the usual problems of reflexive research so well described by Hammersley and Atkinson (1983). Yet no British educational researcher has yet approached the satisfying reflexive sociological accounts of actors, in this case children's culture, that Silvers (1975) has written. Indeed, there have been no systematic phenomenological accounts by British educational researchers.

The presence of observational and interview data is not necessarily indicative that the research is empiricist or interpretive, nor does the type of data concomitant with an aspiration to contribute to positivistic or constructionist theory. The well known studies of Sharp and Green (1975), and King (1978), like that of Bennett (1976), do not ask teachers (or pupils) directly about purpose, intention or experience. The researchers do not try to pursue the reflexive question 'if I made this interpretation, how have the actors seen it?'.

In the case of Sharp and Green, and King, inferences are made from teachers' utterances and from documentary evidence to construct a set of ideals which the teacher and/or school would claim as principles for practice. We are not criticizing the assumptions that underlie that part of the research: multiple sources are required to discover the avowed, yet often discrepant, purposes of any organization. Unlike the case study work (passim) and that of Silvers (passim), Sharp and Green, and King, having established to their own satisfaction these ideals, pursue only one sort of discrepancy in teachers' schools' practices, the discrepancy which is contrary to the ideals.

The discrepancy between emic and etic accounts is not pursued, making these researches like empiricist studies. Nor are the means of analysis made explicit (as with the progressive focusing or the constant comparative). In our view the data about ideals meets the theories that the authors espouse but discrepancies in the data on practice are not pursued[2] nor are details of informers provided as they are, for instance, in a study by Hamilton (1977) where apparent discrepancies between ideals and practices are pursued over time with one teacher.

Sharp and Green, and King, do not allow teachers' statements of insight into the discrepancies between their ideals and their practices. Their actors are unreflexive about their own condition. They swallow the rhetoric unconditionally and unreflexively, practising teaching and schooling which denies the ideals. Studies like Sharp and Green, and King, deny the possibility that the teachers theorize as much as they, as researchers, do, although within different realms of discourse with different sources of significance. There are now many studies which pursue the discrepancies between and across actors' categories (those of case study [passim], Hamilton [passim]).

The assumptions of unreliability and validity of actors' accounts seem to arise from two sources: from extreme interpretation of Malinowski's (1922) statement:

> 'that the sociologist who relied solely on native informants'
> point of view obtains at best that lifeless body of laws,

regulations, morals and conventionalities; which ought to be obeyed, but in reality are often only evaded. For in actual life rules are never entirely conformed to and it remains the most difficult but indispensable part of the ethnographer's work, to ascertain the extent and mechanism of the deviation';

or from certain Marxist interpretations of the individual in relation to social structure, in which the actors' accounts are considered to be a manifestation of false consciousness. Such researchers who use the methods of interview, observation and what they claim as participant observation only deny their similarity to the empiricist approach but by ignoring the validity of actors' accounts, they are in their theoretical analysis similar to positivists in those respects. There is another position which we believe is untenable for researchers who inevitably deal with the empirical in some form; that it is impossible to give anything like adequate accounts of other persons' views. This is a position from Winch's philosophy (1958) rather than from any tradition of fieldwork research whether empiricist or interpretive.

Acknowledging the need to pursue discrepancy between actors' and observers' accounts and to maintain a self-questioning reflexive perspective, the interpretive researcher asks questions like 'Why am I doing this research?', 'Why on these topics?', 'What are the antecedents to my work?', 'What might be the consequences for those I am studying?'. These are questions which tend to foster a concern with the historical and with policy. Whilst all researchers are accountable for their work, the interpretive researcher, through such questions, becomes more responsible to the wider community of interests than either the academic community or the funding bodies.

Although knowledge and understanding of history and policy may be more characteristic of researchers who pursue discrepancy between observers' and actors' accounts, interest in history and policy is not confined to those researching in the interpretive paradigm. Our view is that the empiricist researcher is led to maintain a separation between the phenomena being studied and his or her own method and practices.

The lack of pursuit of discrepancies even across etic data of, for instance, the Oracle project (Galton *et al*, 1980), and of *Teaching Styles and Pupil Progress* (Bennett, 1976) and the substantial critiques of this form of superficial ahistorical, acontextual research, (McIntyre, 1978; Hamilton and Delamont, 1976; Walker and Adelman, 1975), has done little to limit either this form of research or funds for its support.

One of the assumed outcomes of such research is that a

combination of behavioural categories could be developed that would define a good teacher or a 'good school' (Rutter, 1979). The consequences of the application of such normative specification linked, for instance, to merit payment, promotion and even security of employment are not taken as their responsibility by such empiricist researchers.[3] The Bennett (1976) and Rutter (1979) examples are cases in point.[4] Indeed, no agreed relationship between research and policy has become established in spite of the promise of the various reports and subsequent debates on schooling during the 1960s and 1970s. I.Q. testing, so thoroughly refuted in the 1960s, is being resumed, (albeit under new guises; and in some areas never ceased). Memorization continues to be the desired outcome of most pedagogy. Anxiety of learners is, if anything, being raised. The possibility that formal education will disgorge further generations of academically successful, stable, neurotic introverts, narrowly successful in competitive public examinations, but making few positive contributions to life enhancement, has been left in abeyance. These are some of the unaddressed issues in terms of policy and practice that are the residues of educational research of the last twenty, or rather forty, years.

All research is based on the assumption that careful, systematic enquiry into a publicly acknowledged, valid problem will be seriously considered by policy makers and others with influence in educational matters. That assumption has little to support it. Educational research by and large is ignored or taken up within political expediences. It rarely informs or extends public debate.

The gap in understanding between empiricists and those who give actors' accounts as much validity as observers' accounts, appears unbridgeable. The two types of research are done for different purposes, largely for different audiences and seek different sources of publication. Crucially they differ in terms of what they would consider counting as a significant piece of research. In principle, the empiricist type would value research of high statistical reliability which clearly refuted or confirmed existing hypotheses. For the interpretive type significant work would claim a validity through careful description and analysis. It would pursue discrepancies between observers' and actors' accounts on issues acknowledged as important by the subjects of research themselves.

The relationship of both to practice is, at best, tenuous. The merits of the best interpretive research are that it offers the possibility for both teachers and administrators to open up issues for debate that are too often left unexamined.

Notes

1 Triangulation (Adelman, 1974 and 1981) is one method of exploring the discrepancies between actors' and observers' accounts; it is a method that focuses around very narrow and specific parts of practice, social interaction or an event.
2 It was not disclosed, for instance, that several of the teachers whose accounts are used as data in the Sharp and Green study were probationary.
3 In the USA the consequences of application of such research into the public accountability of teachers and schools has been well documented by, for instance, House (1974) and Wolcott (1977).
4 Gray and Satterley (1981) summarized their several critiques of the Bennett study. The London Institute of Education has published the proceedings of a symposium on the Rutter study. (Tizard, B. *et al* 1980).

References

ADELMAN, C. (1974) 'The Tins', in *Ford Teaching Project,* University of East Anglia, Centre for Applied Research in Education, and 'On first hearing', in ADELMAN, C. (1981) *Uttering, Muttering,* London, Grant McIntyre.

BARNES, D. (1969) *Language, the Learner and the School,* Harmondsworth, Penguin.

BENNETT, N. (1976) *Teaching Styles and Pupil Progress,* Shepton Mallett, Open Books.

CRONBACH, L.J. and SUPPES, P. (Eds) (1969) *Research for Tomorrow's Schools: Disciplined Inquiry for Education,* New York, Macmillan.

DELAMONT, S. (1976) 'Beyond Flanders' Fields. The relationship of subject matter and individuality to classroom style', in STUBBS, M. and DELAMONT, S. *Explorations in Classroom Observation,* London, Wiley.

DELAMONT, S. and HAMILTON, D. (1976) 'Classroom research: a critique and a new approach' in STUBBS, M. and DELAMONT, S. *Explorations in Classroom Observation,* London, Wiley.

GALTON, M., SIMON, B. and CROLL, P. (1980) *Inside the Primary Classroom,* London, Routledge and Kegan Paul.

GLASER, B.G. and STRAUSS, A.L. (1964) 'Awareness content and social interaction', *American Sociological Review,* 29, 5.

GRAY, J. and SATTERLY, D. (1981) 'Formal or informal? A re-assessment of the British evidence', *British Journal of Educational Psychology,* 51, pp. 187–196.

HAMILTON, D. (1977) *In Search of Structure: A Case-Study of a New Scottish Open-plan Primary School,* London, Hodder and Stoughton.

HAMMERSLEY, M. and ATKINSON, P. (1983) *Ethnography: Principles in Practice,* London, Methuen.

HOUSE, E. *et al.* (1974) 'An assessment of the Michigan accountability system', *Phi Delta Kappan,* 55, 10, pp. 663–669.

KING, R. (1978) *All Things Bright and Beautiful? A Sociological Study of Infants' Classrooms.* Chichester. Wiley.

KOGAN, M. (1971) *The Politics of Education*, (Edward Boyle and Anthony Crosland in conversation with Maurice Kogan), Harmondsworth. Penguin.

LEVI-STRAUSS, C. (1968) *Structural Anthropology*, Vol. 2 Harmondsworth, Penguin.

MACDONALD, B., ADELMAN, C., KUSHNER, S., and WALKER, R. (1982) *Bread and Dreams: Bilingual Schooling in Boston*, CARE Occasional Publication No. 12, University of East Anglia.

MACDONALD, B. and WALKER, R. (1975) 'Case study and the social philosophy of educational research', *Cambridge Journal of Education*, 5, pp. 2–11.

MALINOWSKI, B. (1922) *The Sexual Life of Savages*. London, Routledge.

McINTYRE, D. and MACLEOD, G. (1978) 'The characteristics and uses of systematic observation', in McALEESE, R. and HAMILTON, D. *Understanding Classroom Life*, Windsor, NFER Publishing Co.

NEEDHAM, R. (1976) *Moulds of Understanding: A Pattern of Natural Philosophy*, London, Allen and Unwin.

PARLETT, M. and HAMILTON, D. (1972) *Evaluation as Illumination: A New Approach to the Study of Innovatory Programmes*, Occasional Paper 9, University of Edinburgh, Centre for Research in the Educational Sciences.

PIKE, K.L. (1967) *Language in Relation to a Unified Theory of the Structure of Human Behaviour*, The Hague, Mouton.

RESNICK, L.B. (1972) 'Teacher behaviour in the informal classroom', in *Journal of Curriculum Studies*, 4, 2, pp. 99–109.

ROBINSON, W.S. (1969) 'The logical structure of analytic induction' in McCALL, G.J. and SIMMONS, J.C. (Eds.) *Issues in Participant Observation*, Reading, Mass. Addison-Wesley.

RUTTER, M. (1979) *Fifteen Thousand Hours: Secondary Schools and Their Effect on Children*, Shepton Mallet, Open Books.

SHARP, R. and GREEN, A.G. (1975) *Education and Social Control*, London, Routledge and Kegan Paul.

SILVERS, R.J. (1975) 'Deserving children's culture', Paper presented at the Third OISE Research and Development Colloquium: *Everyday Life in Educational Settings.*

SIMONS, H. (Ed.) (1980) *Towards a Science of the Singular. Essays about Case Study in Educational Research and Evaluation.* Occasional Publications No. 10, University of East Anglia, Centre for Applied Research in Education.

TIZARD, B. *et al.* (1980) *Fifteen Hundred Hours — A Discussion*, Bedford Way Papers, No. 1, London, Institute of Education.

TORODE, B. (1976) 'Teachers' talk and classroom discipline', in HARRE, R. (Ed.) *Life Sentences of the Social Role of Language*, Chichester, Wiley, and in STUBBS, M. and DELAMONT, S. *Explorations in Classroom Observation*, London, Wiley.

WALKER, R. (1974) 'The conduct of educational case studies: ethics, theory and procedures', in *SAFARI: Innovation, Evaluation, Research and the Problem of Control, Some Interim Papers*, University of East Anglia, Centre for Applied Research in Education.

WALKER, R. (1978) in STAKE, R.E., EASLEY, J. *et al. Case Studies in Science Education*, Washington, US Government Printing Office, for University of Illinois at Urbana-Champaign, Center for Instructional Research and Curriculum Evaluation (CIRCE) and Committee on Culture and Cognition.

WALKER, R. (1983) 'Three good reasons for not doing case studies in curriculum research', *Journal of Curriculum Studies*, 15, 2, pp. 155–165.

WALKER, R. and ADELMAN, C. (1972) 'Towards a sociology of classrooms' *Final Report to the SSRC* Grants 996/1 and 14427/1, London, Chelsea College.

WALKER, R. and ADELMAN, C. (1975) 'Interaction analysis in informal classrooms: a critical comment of the Flanders system', *British Journal of Educational Psychology*, 45:1, pp. 73–6.

WALKER, R. and ADELMAN, C. (1976) 'Strawberries', in STUBBS, M. and DELAMONT, S., *Explorations in Classroom Observation*, London, Wiley.

WINCH, P. (1958) *The Idea of a Social Science and Its Relation to Philosophy*, New York, Routledge and Kegan Paul.

WOLCOTT, H. (1977) *Teachers versus Technocrats*, Centre for Educational Policy and Management, University of Oregon.

2
Educational Research: Policies and Practices

The Contribution of Research to Decision-Making in Education

Marten Shipman

In this Part the relation between educational research and its potential users is examined. Here the changes in the organization of research outlined in Part 1 are shown to be paralleled by changes in the administration and teaching to which the evidence relates. Drysdale stresses the rush and bustle in the office as education officers cope with reorganization, increased political pressure and diminished resources. Mitchell points to the way teachers are trying to respond to similar developments, particularly in the inner cities. Both look to research for help in these efforts, stressing the scarcity of information for decision-making in office and school. Bennett and Desforges detail the variety in contemporary efforts to apply research to schooling and to ensure practical outcomes. But they stress the limitations of such applied research in the absence of understanding about the processes involved. In the end, decision-maker and researcher ask 'why', because however useful it is to know what is going on, acting to improve it requires some understanding of the forces involved.

Behind this second Part, and closely related to Chapters 1 to 4, is an uncomfortable change in the status of social science research in general in its relation to policy-making. Educational researchers have been caught up in the consequences of a widespread acknowledgement of the limitations of social research. They have been especially vulnerable because their work tends to rest on other social sciences, particularly Psychology and Sociology. The internecine disputes in these subjects have not only weakened the combatants, but have alerted the bystanders in DES, town and county hall, and in schools, that any evidence can be challenged, not only on technical grounds, but as politically biased.

By the 1980s the research community in Education was depress-
ed. Summarizing this feeling is part of the Preface to a conference
organized by the Netherlands Foundation for Educational Research
in 1981, which involved leading policy-oriented educational researchers from the UK, USA, Europe and Scandinavia (Kallen *et al,*
1982).

> As the volume of policy-oriented research mounted, how-
> ever, so did feelings of unease about its rationale. To date no
> more than scattered instances are on record of research having
> had an immediately demonstrable impact on public policies.
> The initial sanguine expectations that the social sciences
> would provide a solid groundwork on which to base policy
> decisions and evaluations have not been fulfilled.

The response of the policy-makers who provided the money for the
research was similar in all the countries represented. They bound
researchers into a customer-contractor relationship to ensure that the
work was relevant. But that was anathema to the researchers for it
not only restricted their professional freedom, it inhibited their
search for the theories and models that would lead to the understanding that could really inform policy. Long-term benefits from research
were being sacrificed for short-term data that was itself diminished in
value by being divorced from its theoretical roots.

Thus accompanying the shift of methods described in Part 1 has
been a parallel decline in the prestige of researchers as advisers in
policy formation. This has been accelerated by the success of
researchers themselves in spreading knowledge about research and in
promoting school-based work. The research process has been suc-
cessfully demystified. However, the demand for research to inform
policy remains surprisingly strong. Those who make decisions,
whether at central or local government level or in schools and
colleges, are always short of information and of ways of thinking
about issues. To understand this co-existence of strong criticism with
strong demand, three factors will be examined, the process of
demystifying educational research, the differing obligations of researchers and policy-makers, and the non-linear nature of decision-
making and implementation. Each of these partially accounts for the
current strengths and weaknesses of educational research and jointly
they point to the reasons behind recent changes in the organization,
location and funding of programmes.

The Demystification of Research

It is now conventional to point to the 1970s as a watershed in education, separating the sweet from the hard life. However historically myopic that view, there was increased public criticism. So there was of educational research and this was exacerbated by fratricide. It was this period that witnessed the public attack on quantitative methods documented in Part 1. In particular, these focused on three projects justifiably described as the most influential and controversial of these years (Radical Statistics Education Group, 1982). These were *Teaching Styles and Pupil Progress* (Bennett, 1976), *Fifteen Thousand Hours* (Rutter, 1979) and *Progress in Secondary Schools* (Steedman, 1980) and the response to this National Children's Bureau report from the Centre for Policy Studies (Cox and Marks, 1980). In each case there was a combination of technical and political dispute. It was not just the inadequacies in method that were exposed, but the ease with which bias could be built into research design and the analysis of data. The three disputes, following each other within four years at a time of intense debate about education in general, showed the public and the paymasters not only disagreement, but buffoonery (Shipman, 1981).

These three episodes are well documented and were headline news even in the popular press. *Teaching Styles and Pupil Progress* was the subject of an entire Horizon programme on the day of publication. It generated a dispute among the research community that was at least as sensational as that in the popular press (Shipman, 1981). In a reanalysis of the data Aitkin, Bennett and Hesketh (1981) arrived at very different conclusions from the 1976 original. The episode sapped the confidence of users of research. An equally bitter and even more documented dispute followed the publication of *Fifteen Thousand Hours*. There are two booklets of criticism and defence (Tizard *et al*, 1980 and Wragg *et al*, 1980), probing into assumptions, methods and statistical analysis. In this case the bewilderment of policy-makers was greater because the book seemed to suggest not only that schools could be effective, but the factors behind that effectiveness. That gave them hope after a generation of evidence showing the overwhelming influence of social background on attainment (Gray, 1981). But that turned to despair as the critics began to bite.

Progress in Secondary Schools was one of a series of reports from the National Children's Bureau based on the National Child Development Study. It came to the conclusion that pupil progress in comprehensive and selective schls was similar. It was followed by a swingeing critique from the Centre for Policy Studies (Cox and Marks, 1980). The debate that followed was fought out in the national press and involved the DES statisticians, the Secretary of State, the academic critics (Gray, 1981) and a vigorous counter-attack by the NCB (Steedman, Fogelman and Hutchison, 1980). The British Educational Research Association was roused to criticize Cox and Marks for 'language and tone which went beyond what is normally acceptable' (British Educational Research Association, 1981). But by then the damage was done. At the start of the 1980s there was every incentive for researchers to avoid the quantitative research that would expose them to another barrage from awaiting professional critics, while there was equal incentive for government and the funding bodies for research to view the enterprise with a jaundiced eye.

Thus it is important to go beyond both methodological issues and financial constraint to understand the emerging relation between educational research and policy-making in the 1980s. There was also a demystification (Irvine, Miles and Evans, 1979). This freed researchers from a compulsion to concentrate on quantitative methods. But it meant not only that the switch to ethnography came just as resources became scarce, but just as those who paid for the research community were disillusioned over the results from their earlier investment and in possession of the critical tools to dissect new proposals.

The Obligations of Researchers and Policy-Makers

At the start of the 1970s Lord Rothschild recommended that government, in providing money for research, should also play a major part in selecting and defining the issues to be investigated (Rothschild, 1971). This customer/contractor principle has lain behind recent policies for research, particularly that funded by the Social Science Research Council and directly by the DES. This shift seems to have been international (Kallen *et al*, 1982). Governments worldwide have restricted the scope of researchers, even in the social sciences, which in the UK receive under five per cent of total funds allocated to the research councils and distributed by the renamed Economic and Social Research Council.

Despite the disillusionment with research in the education service it remains influential. One of the triumphs has been that the research techniques and criteria are now in widespread use by inspectors, advisors, teachers and lecturers. Indeed, to survey or to distribute a questionnaire is now commonplace. As these techniques have been discarded within the scientific community, they have been adopted outside. The dependence on research arises firstly from the scarcity of information available when decisions have to be made in central or local government, school, college or classroom. Research, broadly defined, is an everyday office activity. A Chairman will ask officers to brief him or her. A CEO or AEO will instruct a junior to collect data and report back. A Chief Inspector may organize a survey or ask for a quick collection of opinions.

The content of this description and evaluation that is the everyday activity in the office is largely concerned with opportunity costs. If this action is taken, that cannot be. The question asked is usually about cost-effectiveness which is rarely in the mind of the researcher. Inevitably decisions in education involve balancing the benefits of this action against alternatives. Yet that is far from the minds of researchers. For example, in all the published accounts of Schools Council project evaluations, there is no mention of costs. Yet that is uppermost for the policy-maker.

At the heart of the problems of harnessing the potential of research to decision-making lie the two audiences facing researchers. Allegiance can be to the administration of education, but is more likely to be to the research community itself and to the academic institutions within which researchers work and see their futures. It is not just that this community serves as the main reference for researchers because it is where their support and future lies. What matters is the way the communal structures and norms differ from that in educational administration. The consequences of these differences are more than a problem of communication. There are two separate reward-systems and this creates problems for all researchers, but particularly for those who have moved from quantitative to qualitative research styles.

Even within a research community it is difficult to appreciate the sanctions that constrain both junior and senior. Research is the most important criterion for academic promotion. It is important in the completion of probation as a lecturer and for passing through the efficiency bar in a university. Publication is the key to success. But publication and the judgment of the quality of research are controlled by senior academics. They edit the journals, advise the publishers, referee the articles, externally examine theses, dissertations and examinations. They serve on appointment panels and give references to those seeking posts. Publication in a respected refereed journal is a mark of acceptance and often the key to an appointment or to promotion. It is controlled and, as a result, the inferior is seen to be rejected and what is to count as valid evidence is accepted. Those trying to establish a research career, or a successful academic career, in education or the social sciences are expected to attend conferences, join networks, know who is doing what and to satisfy academic criteria of excellence. This is not just the avenue to promotion. It is the way evidence is given the stamp of approval. Fortunately the disciplines are not unitary. It is possible to find an amenable community where your far-out views on politics or methods of research will be accepted. But in all cases recognition, reward, even obtaining an audience, depend on satisfying senior academics in often tight-knit groups which have their own language, theoretical frameworks and methodologies.

In a similar way, administrators, inspectors and teachers have similar obligations and audiences that provide recognition of the worth of activities. When Her Majesty's Inspectors published *Primary Education in England* (DES, 1978) it was clear that they had adopted the standardized form of data collection that had previously been the technique of academic researchers. But it is also clear that in this and later surveys (DES, 1979, 1982 and 1983) Inspectors were continuing their responsibility to recommend as well as report, set priorities as well as establish a data base. In adopting this prescriptive as well as descriptive role they were only doing overtly what many researchers do covertly. But the Inspectors were also collecting information on the state of the different age phases of schooling and providing politicians and administrators with an account of the way resources were being spent. It would be absurd to criticize these HMI surveys for being uncritical of policy or unconcerned with problems of inequality or injustice. The obligations of HMI are to monitor and influence the service as an integral but independent part of its government. They form their own community with their own responsibilities and authority structure. It is these rather than technical differences over methods that distinguish HMI surveys from similar data collection by researchers. Similarly teachers have adopted research methods, particularly in evaluating their own efforts, but they too design the work and evaluate its worth by reference to their fellow teachers.

The puzzled politician reading a research report that seems to be simple observations dressed up in a language described as ethnography or phenomenology is in a similar position to a teacher bewildered by the apparent insensitivity of the administrator who refers to nationally falling pupil-teaching ratios when the problem is the loss of the only modern linguist in the school, or the researcher suspicious of the absence of detail about sampling in HMI surveys. Each has obligations to different reference groups which are the source of social and material rewards and which provide a shared way of viewing and analyzing the world.

The Complexity of Decision-Making and Implementation

The model of decision-making and implementation used by researchers tends to be linear. Someone Great and Good spells it out, administrators work out the details, office staff and then teachers put it into practice. The link from policy statement to its implementation is seen as passive as the administration works out procedures. This model is in line with textbook versions of bureaucracy. But in practice policies are interpreted and adapted at every stage. Nor are these adaptations necessarily rational. Indeed, the initial policy may itself be less of a calculated consideration of alternatives than an effort to cope with a situation where the costs and the benefits of actions could not even be defined. Thus instead of a linear series of planned decisions based on a rational consideration of alternative actions, there is usually a bustle of decisions made at all levels of administration. Influences percolate up as well as down. Arbitrary changes in plans are made to fit procedures to cases that don't match them. Policies get made and are implemented, but through improvization and adjustment. That is why an organization such as the Assessment of Performance Unit slowly but steadily changes from a monitoring to a curriculum-focused mode of working. The recognition of this non-linear and often confusing path to decision-making is crucial to understanding the place of research (Weiss and Bucuvalas, 1980).

Mirroring the conventional if misleading linear and rational model of decision-making is a linear model for policy-orientated research. The researcher was assumed to provide evidence on the policy alternatives and to help in the making of the optimal decisions. The issues were received, defined, researched and reported on as if there were single sources of decision. If the process of deciding and implementing policies is incremental and often diffused throughout a service such as Education, a different model for utilizing research is necessary. There is an obvious parallel with the history of curriculum research. In the 1960s it was assumed that the sequence was Research — Development — Application. The university-based project would produce a seedbed for the school to harvest. In practice it became clear that if research was to be influential it had to affect practice at many different levels, not only in central and local government, School Council and advisory service, but in headteacher's study, common room and classroom in some 30,000 schools and colleges where incremental policy-making was flourishing.

The situation in the 1980s may not however match that of more expansive decades. As the location of influence changes, so may the optimum point for research. For example, financial constraint tends to push the location of power towards the centre (Fowler, 1979). Schools await decisions on staffing or curriculum from county or town hall because they are unsure of their forthcoming resources. But, in turn, LEAs await decisions within their parent authority once the grant from the centre has been decided. The place for curriculum research in the 1960s may have been in the schools, but with curriculum-led staffing in the 1980s it may be most profitably focused on LEA staffing policies. Furthermore, it is not just that the location of decisions shifts, but that the impact is differentially felt at the various levels of the service. The same apparent issue may look very different in classroom, common room, headteacher's study, town or county hall, or the DES. Falling national pupil-teacher ratios for example still leave very difficult problems in individual schools and major issues between teacher unions and administration in the LEAs (Shipman, 1984).

The need for a more complex model of the relation of research to policy-making and implementation arises partly out of evidence on the utilization of research. In the USA, Caplan, Morrison and Stambaugh (1975) found that the Office of Education was the government agency most likely to fund policy-related research, but least likely to use it. The literature on the relation between researchers and policy-makers is replete with the need for 'linkages', 'gap-filling', 'great divides', 'knowledge transfers' and 'utilization policies' (Caplan, 1982). The US National Academy of Science assembled a panel of experts at the request of Congress to report on how to meet the information needs of the US Department of Education (National Academy of Science, 1981). This report focuses on the need to adopt a model where 'throughput' is considered as well as 'input' and 'output' in the organization of the education services. This provides a more realistic model and increases the chance of moving from one-shot, single publication, to a process model stressing the 'life cycle' of evidence within the organizations. Throughout this research on research there remains some optimism, based on the continuing hope among policy-makers that research will provide the right information at the right time and place. Efforts to secure this pay-off are now visible in the way research is being organized in the 1980s.

The Changing Pattern of Applied Research

Changes in the public knowledge of research, the realization that the models for utilzing research in policy-making were too simple and the appreciation of the strength of the contrasting values and commitments of researchers and decision-makers at various levels of the education service have produced changes not only in training for a research career, funding and the contracting of projects, but have diffused the action in a way that could not have been predicted in the 1960s and which is not fully appreciated today. Taylor (1973) could report that educational research had benefited from 'a massive increase in resources' in the sixties to poise it ready to play a central part in decision-making in government and school. The Nuffield Foundation alone had provided over £700,000 per year for educational R and D in the late 1960s. Schools Council, SSRC, Leverhulme, Gulbenkian, Rowntree, Van Leer and Ford Foundations were contributing generously. Yet by 1983, Lawton saw a deterioration in each of the three conditions that Taylor a decade earlier had seen as essential for a successful research enterprise (Lawton, 1983). There was no sympathetic political, social and educational climate, adequate resources, nor an appropriate organization. But that is to look at the situation of the professionals. When the total research scene is looked at it is less a deterioration than a transformation.

The first feature of applied research in the 1980s is its spread throughout the education service. The DES through the Assessment of Performance Unit (APU), HMI through surveys and an increase in now published inspections, the LEAs through the increased numbers of test programmes for monitoring and screening have established expensive research programmes at a time when less money has been made available for academic-based work. The APU is an example of this tendency (Gipps and Goldstein, 1983). By the early 1980s it was costing nearly £1,000,000 per year, and, despite a recent decision to confine test programmes to Mathematics, Science and Language and to cease annual monitoring, will remain a major demand on DES funds and on the National Foundation for Educational Research to which much of the work has been contracted. This APU monitoring, particularly in Science, relates performance to school and contextual factors, moving on to territory previously occupied by academic researchers. In the forthcoming years more resources will also be given to further analysis of the data already collected.

Another flourishing activity involves LEA administrators, inspectors and advisers in test programmes. There was only a brief lull after the phasing out of much testing for selection at the end of primary schooling, before LEAs increased their screening and monitoring. Evidence from the Evaluation of Testing in Schools Project, funded by SSRC from 1980 to 1982, shows not only intense, but increased activity (Gipps, Steadman, Blackstone and Stierer, 1983). New test programmes were introduced during the 1970s, with 1978 as the year of most new initiatives. The number of programmes continued to increase across the life of the Project. Behind the increase was pressure from Education Committees for information on standards. Little of this testing has a research as distinct from a diagnostic and accounting purpose, but it used up resources at a time of scarcity and made access more difficult for the academic research community as teachers responded to LEA requests for cooperation.

Probably the most influential development has been the involvement of teachers in research connected activities. The 1970s were a period when the increased number of in-service courses containing a research element and a dissertation coincided with a lack of mobility in the teaching force. Many teachers were in a position to become researchers in their own institutions. This was encouraged by a stress on the value of school-based research (Nixon, 1981) and on school-based curriculum development and evaluation (Elliott, 1980). It was pressed further by the introduction of self-evaluation schemes by LEAs. In 1980, a survey showed sixty-nine of the 104 LEAs involved in discussions about self-evaluation with their teachers. Twenty-one had already published self-evaluation schemes. They ranged from voluntary to mandatory (Oxfordshire) with a large number being used as a basis for in-service courses (Elliott, 1981). The build-up, starting in 1973 and peaking in 1979–80, continued into the 1980s, coinciding with the increase in LEA testing and APU activity.

When this central and local government activity and school-based research and development enterprise is added up it amounts to an important if amateur addition to the work done in professional research organizations and in academia. The diffusion has been encouraged by the Schools Council switching its funding from large projects to local initiatives often involving teachers, and by the publication of new journals such as *School Organization* that encourage teachers to publish their work. Many ambitious examples can be found in the Open University Course E 364 *Curriculum Evaluation and Assessment in Educational Institutions* (Open University, 1983). As this activity was encouraged, the funding for large-scale research was cut. The balance of applied research is being radically altered.

The new situation for professional researchers can be illustrated by changes at the Social Science Research Council. First, the term Science was removed by the Secretary of State and it was renamed the Economic and Social Research Council in 1983. Its funds were cut and changes made both in the training arrangements and in funding. Both of these changes continued trends from the 1970s. First, training awards were opened to direct competition between students in 1984 instead of awards being allocated to academic departments. Second, more awards were to be allocated through collaborative or linked schemes. Collaborative (CASS) awards were to involve students in research in an institution collaborating with a department in higher education. The applications in Education linked the departments with LEAs, schools, welfare agencies, social service departments, examination boards and so on, thus reinforcing the diffusion of research activity. Linked awards placed the student into ongoing research programmes. These awards were being increased while the conventional studentships were reduced.

The basis for funding research has changed only slowly since the Rothschild Report (1971). The customer/contractor principle is more visible in the funding policy of central government departments such as DES. Nevertheless, ESRC has tried to direct research to areas seen as important for policy. The best current example is the Inner City in Context research programme which was to receive £500,000 over three years and which had been funded by over £300,000 within six months of its announcement in August 1982. This was directly designed to improve public policies for the inner cities. This involved designing all the projects within a common research framework, which identified policy objectives, their limits, alternative costs and problems of implementation. Similar, if less sophisticated, attempts to gear research to important policy issues were made in education with money being allocated to programmes on accountability. The crucial change was from responding to applications from researchers to identifying important areas and then asking for bids from the academic community. Alongside this policy, many major projects were funded to illuminate key policy areas. For example, a major commitment for the SSRC across the 1970s and into the 1980s was to a collaborative project on school leavers in Scotland in which the Scottish Education Department cooperated with the Centre for

Educational Sociology at Edinburgh (Gray, McPherson and Raffe, 1983). Significantly this involved the establishment of a data-base for use by administrators, inspectors and teachers.

It is when a synoptic view of the contemporary research scene is taken that the shift to a more policy-orientated, diffused pattern can be seen. Financial constraint may have encouraged such a shift from academia, but there were other factors. These are closely related to the disillusionment with research and the difficulty in getting academic researchers to accept the constraints of policy-orientated work. Indeed, any sustained attempt to merge theory- and policy-orientated research would be a mistake, weakening both. One looks for the innovatory and the iconoclastic, the other for the dependable and the context, cost-bound evaluatory. They complement each other, but a merger could compromise the detached critic and deflect the in-house worker. The division of labour in educational research is becoming clearer in the 1980s. The diffusion of effort is as much a sign of success in spreading the value of research as it is of weakness in satisfying the paymasters.

References

AITKIN, M.A., BENNETT, S.N. and HESKETH, J. (1981) 'Teaching styles and pupil progress; a re-analysis', *British Journal of Educational Psychology*, 51, pp. 170–86.

BENNETT, S.N. (1976) *Teaching Styles and Pupil Progress*, London, Open Books.

BRITISH EDUCATIONAL RESEARCH ASSOCIATION (1981) Editorial statement, *Research Intelligence*, April, p. 1.

CAPLAN, N. (1982) 'Social research and public policy at the national level', in KALLEN, D.B.P. *et al.*, *Social Science Research and Public Policy-Making*, London, Nelson.

CAPLAN, N., MORRISON, A. and STAMBAUGH, R. (1975) *The Use of Social Science Knowledge in Policy Decisions at the National Level*, Ann Arbor, Institute for Social Research, University of Michigan.

COX, C. and MARKS, J. (1980) *Real Concern: an Appraisal of the National Children's Bureau Report on 'Progress in Secondary Schools'*, London, Centre for Policy Studies.

DEPARTMENT OF EDUCATION AND SCIENCE (1978) *Primary Education in England and Wales*, London, HMSO.

DEPARTMENT OF EDUCATION AND SCIENCE (1979) *Aspects of Secondary Education in England*, London, HMSO.

DEPARTMENT OF EDUCATION AND SCIENCE (1982) *Education 5 to 9: an illustrative survey of 80 First Schools in England*, London, HMSO.

DEPARTMENT OF EDUCATION AND SCIENCE (1983) *9–13 Middle Schools: an Illustrative Survey*, London, HMSO.

ELLIOTT, G. (1981) *Self-Evaluation and the Teacher*, Hull, University of Hull/Schools Council.

ELLIOTT, J. (1980) *SSRC Cambridge Accountability Project: A Summary Report*, Cambridge, Cambridge Institute of Education, mimeograph.

FOWLER, G. (1979) 'The politics of education' in BERNBAUM, G. (Ed.) *Schooling in Decline*, Basingstoke, Macmillan.

GIPPS, C. and GOLDSTEIN, H. (1983) *Monitoring Children*, London, Heinemann.

GIPPS, C., STEADMAN, S., BLACKSTONE, T. and STIERER, B. (1983) *Testing Children*, London, Heinemann.

GRAY, J. (1981) 'Towards effective schools: problems and progress in British research', *British Educational Research Journal*, 7, 1, pp. 187–196.

GRAY, J., McPHERSON, A.F. and RAFFE, D. (1983) *Reconstructions of Secondary Education*, London, Routledge and Kegan Paul.

IRVINE, J., MILES, I. and EVANS, J. (Eds.) (1979) *Demystifying Social Statistics*, London, Pluto Press.

KALLEN, D.B.P. *et al.* (1982) *Social Science Research and Public Policy-Making*, London, Nelson.

LAWTON, D. (1983) 'The politics of educational research', *Times Educational Supplement*, 9.9.83. p. 4.

NATIONAL ACADEMY OF SCIENCE (1981) *Program Evaluation in Education*, Washington DC.

NIXON, J. (Ed.) (1981) *A Teachers' Guide to Action Research*, London, Grant McIntyre.

OPEN UNIVERSITY (1983) *Curriculum Evaluation and Assessment in Educational Institutions*, E364 Milton Keynes, Open University Press.

RADICAL STATISTICS EDUCATION GROUP (1982) *Reading Between the Numbers*, London, BSSRS Publications.

ROTHSCHILD REPORT (1971) *A Framework for Government Research and Development*, Cmnd 4814, London, HMSO.

RUTTER, M. *et al.* (1979) *Fifteen Thousand Hours*, London, Open Books.

SHIPMAN, M.D. (1981) *The Limitations of Social Research*, London, Longman.

SHIPMAN, M.D. (1984) *Education as a Public Service*, London, Harper and Row.

STEEDMAN, J. (1980) *Progress in Secondary Schools*, London, National Children's Bureau.

STEEDMAN, J., FOGELMAN, K. and HUTCHISON, D. (1980) *Real Research: a Rebuttal of Allegations*, London, National Children's Bureau.

TAYLOR, W. (1973) 'The organization of educational research in the United Kingdom', in TAYLOR, W. (Ed.) *Research Perspectives in Education*, London, Routledge and Kegan Paul.

TIZARD, B. *et al.* (1980) *15,000 Hours: A Discussion*, London, University of London, Institute of Education, Bedford Way Papers.

WEISS, C.H. and BUCUVALAS, M.J. (1980) *Social Science Research and Decision-Making*, New York, Columbia University Press.

WRAGG, E. *et al.* (1980) *The Rutter Research*, Exeter, University of Exeter, School of Education.

Research and the Education Administrator

Dennis H. Drysdale

The tenor and emphasis of local government administration, and particularly education administration, has changed considerably in the last decade. The change roughly coincides with local government reorganization in 1974, though it only partly resulted from it. In the shire counties in particular reorganization brought with it a tendency towards the greater influence of party politics on local government, resulting mainly from the shotgun marriages between largely non-political former counties and the much more political county boroughs and excepted districts. The heightened party political rivalry led the parties to adopt a more accountable stance towards their electorates, and this, together with the keen and constant competition between them, led to increased demands on administrators by their political masters, greater urgency to meet more frequent deadlines, constant pressure on staffing levels and resource constraints which made it less and less possible to take educational decisions on educational grounds.

The change of professional life-style for education administrators at this time, however, could not be attributed either wholly or even mainly to reorganization, but was much more the result of the changing economic order from the never-had-it-so-good era to the descent into recession. The first real manifestation of trouble was the oil crisis of the early seventies, with which both politicians and administrators at all levels of government were just beginning to struggle when the new shadow authorities were elected in 1973. They have been struggling with subsequent economic events ever since and would have had to do so whether or not there had been any reorganization. Similarly, the greater influence of party politics on local government would, I think, have occurred without reorganization, largely as a result of the continuing economic crisis, since during times when resources are scarce, the debate on their uses becomes more intense, and that implies more political activity. Reorganization certainly aided the process in that where non-political county authorities were merged with much more politically controlled county boroughs there was a tendency for the experienced party politicians in the boroughs to gain control of the new authority and establish mini-Westminster styles of government. But even where reorganization did not immediately have this effect, the party system with its group meetings, whips and powerful committee chairmen drawn from the inner caucus of the majority party seems to have gradually evolved, largely in response to economic pressures. Now indeed, a number of local politicians and local government groupings are becoming much more prominent in national politics and decision making; ACC, AMA and CLEA, for instance, are more effective in influencing central government thinking than their predecessors, and personalities like Beryl Platt, Alastair Lawton, Nicky Harrison and David Blunkett have been able remarkably quickly to achieve national prominence from their power bases in local government.

Before the mid-seventies, when administration was one of the career choices open to ambitious educationalists, educational research was a tool of the trade, potentially important to the judgment of administrators in formulating policy proposals, and time could be found to consider both the findings and the rationale of projects which addressed themselves to current problems. Since reorganization, there has been little time to reflect on the results of research and even less to study the detail, however topical. Ironically, therefore, at a time when administrators are desperately in need of all available professional help, they turn less than ever to potentially one of its best sources.

This picture may be over simplified, but it is no less indicative for that, and it implies an important message for researchers as well as administrators, since just as the external pressures of the last decade have made it difficult for administrators to reflect on and use the most appropriate basis for their decisions or proposals, so the same pressures have discovered major weaknesses in the nature and quality of educational research, and in its ability to make its proper contribution just at the time when it could most benefit the education service it exists to support, a time of social changes so significant that all the personal social services are having to be rethought, hastily, yet without those responsible being able to see clearly the circumstances these revised services will have to meet.

Dennis H. Drysdale

The events of recent years have required the administrators in all these services to come to terms with a new professional style, resilient enough to meet the combined and relatively sudden challenge of a number of pressures hitherto either unknown to them or experienced in only a more transient, less intense form. The most fundamental has been the persistence of the economic recession, which has not been the periodic, short-lived form of recession with which management in general has largely been able to cope, but a recession born of the transition through which Western communities are passing from one economic era to another. Not only is this phenomenon new to us all, not only are its results severe and in many ways virtually permanent, but in trying in spite of everything to maintain the provision of an education service which is relevant and of high quality on ever decreasing resources, administrators are faced with nagging doubts about objectives, since none of us is quite sure of the nature and demands of the society for which we are preparing the users of the service, whether they be young people or adults seeking to adapt to the new era through continuing education. We are not, of course, the only ones disorientated by this period of transition; so are our political masters, so are our clients and so are the parents of our schoolchildren. All of them look to 'the professionals' in the service, of which the administrators are one group, to relieve in varying degrees their doubts or fears, and our performance is under continual scrutiny. All of a sudden, the pressure of life at the top has become an uncomfortable fact, not something belonging to another world which we glimpsed only through fiction of TV soap opera. In these circumstances 'administration' becomes a dirty word, synomymous with 'waste of scarce resources', but sound, imaginative, well-informed administration is vital to the survival of a civilized society, and it is in seeking to provide the administration behind the education service our society needs now, and will need in the new economic situation, that education administrators need all the professional allies available, including research.

The problems with which administrators are faced when seeking assistance from educational research arise in simple terms from the fact that while administrators are already, and of necessity, adapting fast to their new task, many researchers seem less ready to appreciate that long established research traditions and methods no longer meet the needs of many professional colleagues who could still draw great benefit from their skills if they were adapted to meet current circumstances. For instance, some of the main characteristics of research might be said to be:—

1   in depth studies of issues of interest, often mainly for their own sake or their own intrinsic merit, rather than for real practical purposes;
2   the devizing of detailed investigations, experiments and control systems in order to test hypotheses and validate conclusions;
3   the presentation of results in complicated, analytical forms, requiring time and specialist knowledge to read.

Against this the basic tasks of the education administrator today are:—

1   to keep abreast of developments in a service which is changing and developing faster than ever in response to political, economic and social pressures;
2   to evaluate these developments in terms of local services and propose or take action accordingly;
3   to seek to maintain a realistic service of real quality in the face of resource constraints and radical changes in the reasonable expectations of young people completing their education;
4   to plan as far as constraints allow, or react logically, knowledgeably and professionally when there is no time to plan;
5   to do all the above in accordance with tight time scales dictated by deadlines over which he has little control.

Inevitably, therefore, the administrator finds himself in a position where he desperately needs readily available intelligence of a kind which can be provided, *inter alia,* by research, but turns less and less to research for it because he cannot allow himself the luxury of trying to pick the concealed bones out of the minute detail and abstruse modes of expression in the research documents which come his way, much though he might have enjoyed the intellectual exercise in other circumstances.

Yet there may never be a time when research could have provided a more valuable service to education administrators and to their authorities. In recent years, for instance, administrators have had to propose sensible solutions at short notice to such problems as falling rolls (and the general management of contraction), effective provision for the handicapped (integration or segregation?), workable comprehensive reorganization (middle schools, eleven to eighteen, tertiary, sixth form colleges?), the retraining of staff for redeployment, the management of large institutions which devour scarce resources, valid and realistic forms of government for schools or colleges, school-industry liaison linked with the preparation of young people for working life, methods of evaluating and assessing educational achievement and curriculum development in various forms, to name but a few current headaches. In developing effective policies on all of these issues, the findings of imaginative and reliable research could be of great value, and could, if only by setting them thinking right from the start along fruitful lines, save administrators much time and frustration, as well as lending some reliability to their conclusions.

The problem is sometimes the complete lack of relevant research, but much more frequently the necessary documentation is available through agencies ranging from university education departments through specialist research bodies attached to universities (like the Institute of Manpower Studies at Sussex University) to bodies set up expressly to service education (National Foundation for Educational Research, Schools Council, Council for Educational Technology). The real problem therefore is that the available research is rejected by administrators either because it is indigestible, at least in the time available, or because the project has been perceived from an academic or philosophical point of view rather than from the aspect which would have made it relevant to administrators' needs. So much effort by intelligent researchers with much to offer to the education system is therefore wasted and, even more sadly, anti-research attitudes are developed — negative and illogical attitudes, but understandable nevertheless.

In spite of everything, however, research must go on, its results must be put to good use and the education system and those it exists to serve must be the beneficiaries. It is essential, therefore, to appreciate how research institutions and their staff can identify, carry out and present their exercises in such a way that they may have the effect and value which is their justification. I want to suggest five guiding principles which should underpin any educational research project which is intended to be of use in the administration and management of the service, then to examine some practical implications of these principles and finally to consider in broad terms the position of the relevant research agencies in the light of these implications. I appreciate, of course, that research exists to serve other functions and other audiences from those with whom I am principally concerned here, as Shipman argues in greater detail in his associated article, and that even the education administrator would be unwise to ignore the broader range of critical and prognostic research which impinges on his field, but I believe that it is on practical, utilitarian research that the partnership between administrator and research needs primarily to be founded, hence the emphasis I place on it.

The five guiding principles are:

1   It is essential to select the right projects, those which will make a positive contribution to the thinking which authorities are having to do now or will obviously have to do in the near future.
2   The emphasis in projects should be chosen to reflect the kinds of decision with which authorities (members or officers) are faced.
3   The right people must be chosen to do the research. This may well mean teaming someone with research skills with a partner experienced in education management or administration.
4   The right research methods have to be chosen. In general this means those which will obtain the most reliable results in a time scale which will allow those results, when published, still to have currency.
5   The results must be presented in ways which allow the main conclusions to be readily appreciated together with their implications while still providing the supporting evidence for use as appropriate.

At the root of the whole exercise is the selection of the right project. Ideally, researchers need to be one or two steps ahead of current developments so that the results of their exercises are published just in time to be of evident value to administrators for whom the topic in question has just become a major priority and will remain one for a limited time in the future. A research publication which arrives too late will be ignored for obvious reasons, while one which arrives too early is likely to be shelved for future reference and to have been forgotten by the time it becomes needed. It is not suggested that researchers need to be clairvoyant; careful reading and assessment of the education press and regular consultation with professional bodies such as the Society of Education Officers will indicate with reasonable certainty where the vital lines of enquiry lie.

But it is not simply a question of selecting the right issues; to be of real value, research must pinpoint the aspects of those issues which are really of current concern to administrators. Special education, for instance, can nearly always be a fruitful field, but many of the general principles need little further elaboration, and teaching methods have received much attention for many years now. The Warnock Report and the 1981 Education Act, however, have highlighted a number of issues which are currently high on the list of priorities for education officers responsible for special education, for example integration versus segregation, assessment procedures and a proper range of further education and training opportunities for the handicapped from the age of sixteen onwards. Or again, the problem of managing a contracting education service is one with which hardly any education officer in post today has ever had to deal before, yet effective management decisions are already having to be made, based largely on sheer professional instinct supplemented by such management skills as administrators trained as teachers have been able to acquire on the job. The availability of good, practical, well-presented research in this area could be invaluable.

However skilled a researcher is in the practice of his trade and however knowledgeable he may be about the education process, he is unlikely to be able to produce results of real assistance to administrators unless an experienced administrator gives him the right perspective on his subject and advises, for example, on the kind of indices which would be useful in the results and conclusions. Administrators, on the other hand, may not be good researchers; if they are lucky they do not have to be, since they have junior staff to research for them, but they have to develop a sure eye for the kind of research they need and the kind of information and results they are looking for. The opportunity is there for researchers to call on administrators' skill at identifying topics for examination and angles to pursue, and then to use their own skills to carry out projects which will give back to administrators work of quality and value.

Government in general has developed in style and tenor to meet the demands for instant information, opinion and decision making which stem from a world in which travel and communications have become so easy and so well developed, and in which the media play such a large role. If researchers are to be of real assistance to those involved in government, either as elected representatives or as officers, they must adapt their own methods to the social context in which they are working. Rarely now can they afford the long, deep, multi-controlled look at their subject; sharp, incisive examination is required, based on knowing (probably after taking advice) precisely what information they require and where to find it. News has always had very limited currency, and research is now beginning to face the same problems, at least in the immediate sense, so fast is the pace of modern government, even if the resultant decisions and actions still seem to those outside the corridors of power to take so long to materialize.

The presentation of research findings in readily digestible form is absolutely essential if they are to catch the eye and the attention of the administrator. On top of the reports to prepare, meetings to attend, troubleshooting, routine administration and amateur accountancy which are his lot — not one about which he would generally complain, for it still has variety, interest and a great deal of satisfaction, but one for which there are never enough hours in the day — he is confronted with an ever flowing tide of documentation to read. He tackles the majority either in detail or by using the bone picking skills which are essential to him, but he discards as much as he reasonably feels he can, and may, for no more logical reason than frustration, assume he need not bother about documents the content or import of which is not readily apparent. Sadly, these can often be research documents whose value would have been appreciated had more thought been given to presentation. Research reports should, in broad terms, start with a simple statement of the main aims followed by the main findings, set out in brief and uncomplicated style. Having thus caught the attention of their intended reader, they should go on to set out in some detail, but still in simple terms how the project was conceived and carried out and what was achieved as a result, by which point the administrator will have been able to assess its immediate potential implications for him and his authority, and will already be deciding how to make the best use of it. Then finally, probably in one or more appendices, the real detail of the research should be set out, with its charts, questionnaires, statistical surveys, observations, judgments, tests of hypotheses and so on, still preferably with as little jargon as possible. The likelihood is that if the documentation is presented in this way, with attractive print and graphic layouts, the administrator will read and use it, possibly taking the trouble eventually to read even the detailed appendices, which he will much more readily appreciate since he is already familiar with the context rather than having to deduce it from struggling with the minute detail.

The main implication of all this for research bodies would therefore seem to be:

1   Choose researchers who know the context. However good they are as researchers, they are not likely to be fully effective if their knowledge of their subject at the outset is superficial.

2   Consult those for whom the research is intended before topics and lines of enquiry are chosen. Regular consultation between the Society of Education Officers and the main research agencies would ensure that scarce resources were used to greatest advantage.
3   Try to arrange for someone knowledgeable in the target group to work on the project, for instance by secondment, consultancy arrangements, or the establishment of a support group.
4   Insist that a fundamental skill of the researcher (as perhaps of the administrator) is the ability to present complicated material in simple form and language.
5   Set demanding deadlines for the completion of research, but be prepared to follow up projects which prove useful with further phases developed from reactions to the first phase.
6   Insist that the essential justification for undertaking a project is the utilitarian value of its results rather than the intrinsic interest of the subject to the researcher.

Research then, is a valuable discipline which has the potential to make a significant contribution to effective education administration, and the purpose of these remarks is not to decry research but to encourage researchers to achieve their full potential in this context. The suggested essential message is that researchers should learn their 'three Rs'; their work needs to be relevant, readable and realistic.

Note

The views expressed in this article are personal and do not necessarily reflect the views of the Isle of Wight LEA or the Further Education Unit.

A Teacher's View of Educational Research

Peter Mitchell

Introduction

In writing a paper on a teacher's view of educational research I am immediately made aware of one of the main problems faced by researchers. Teachers, if they give any consideration to research, are normally selective about what they take up. The teaching profession is far from united about the aims and purposes of schools today. This account therefore reflects my own particular concerns.

Educational research comes in a wide variety of forms and determining its relevance to teaching must begin with some knowledge of what a teacher might understand by research. I think there would be a measure of agreement that research should be concerned with improving the intellectual growth and development of children; that it seeks to do this by methods of enquiry which at one extreme attempt to be objective, empirical scientific enquiries, and at the other extreme to be concerned with the detailed participant observation and recording of children learning, teachers teaching and the interrelationships between teachers and children. Both extremes yield hypotheses which may lead to further research. In general teachers would expect large scale empirical research to influence policy makers and small scale classroom research to point directions for their own work. The fact that policy makers ultimately influence classroom practice should not be lost on teachers sensitive to the political nature of educational issues.

Research should be one of the means by which teachers are able to reflect on their work with children. This assumes that the enterprise of teaching is seen as problematic and in need of constant review and questioning. The fact that this is often not the case is to be deplored. The idea that being a subject 'expert' is sufficient preparation for work with children is still influential. This reduces the job of teaching to a series of pragmatic decisions and places teachers on a par with administrators whose making of policy is dominated by the question, 'will it work?' (Work for whom? Work in the short or long term?).

The unifying link between all types of educational enterprise should be a shared concern with improving levels of learning through the provision of experiences which build the individual's confidence in their ability to learn for themselves. One of the preconditions for this is that all educational institutions are seen explicitly as centres where teachers, tutors and lecturers are learning alongside students, whether they be adults or children. Only then will research be seen as an integral part of the practice of schools.

The present is a time when schools and institutions of higher education are experiencing working in a contracting economy. Research in the 1960s was linked to growth and expansion by suggesting ways of developing an educated workforce. At a time of economic expansion it was assumed that an educated workforce would not only lead to more economic growth but also to a more socially just society. The sense of optimism that underpins this consensus view of society's future has now been replaced by insecurity and uncertainty. In the course of this paper I will be attempting to demonstrate that the work of schools needs the involvement of research if they are to come to a fresh understanding of the aims of their work; now is not a time for nurturing divisions within the world of education but for cooperation, in the interest of clients of all ages.

The Traditional View of Educational Research

To most teachers research is an activity carried out by people in higher education in order to acquire a research degree, or in order to fulfil a contract made with an LEA, or the DES. The research may extend longitudinally over a number of years and may involve the collection and analysis of statistical data. Data collection will be within certain categories. Concepts used will have been analyzed and their meaning clarified. The process of scientific enquiry may yield generalizations which can help predict the outcome of future work undertaken by teachers in their classrooms, or provide empirical evidence on which policy decisions are based.

This mechanistic view of research has a natural tendency to exclude the interest and involvement of teachers. The conclusions of the research may give a deceptively over-simplified view of the research and its findings and as a consequence it will tend to be embraced by those whose practices it confirms and rejected by those whose work it appears to question. It is the complexity of the methodology which prevents teachers from being in a position to question the findings. (This complexity may in part be explained by the educationists' search for status within the broad academic world of the university, and it may be this which turns educational research away from the world of teachers.)

Tensions within the research community often centre on the efficacy of scientific methods when used in educational research. Many contributors to this book are critical of the psycho-statistical paradigm. The unease which many teachers feel with this form of research is grounded in much the same concern with people's behaviour being context-bound and therefore resistant to being described by generalizations developed out of empirical research. Schools, classes and individuals are characterized by their unique responses to changes in their circumstances; this does not imply that teachers have any precise understanding of how this occurs or how they should respond collectively or individually to behaviour which is context-bound. Whether presented as an academic critique of quantitative research methods or as the hunch of teachers concerned with the art of their profession, criticism of statistical methods should not distract teachers from the value of this work. It should, for example, be of great interest to teachers to know, from current quantitative research, how much schools vary in the amount of time they devote to particular subjects; how schools vary in the amount of contact time they have with children; how children's attendance relates to their performance in school. This research into contact time and research into teaching styles has been criticized for emphasizing quantity at the expense of quality. Neville Bennett's current research into *The Quality of Pupil Learning Experiences* reflects a change in emphasis but not a change in the direction of his researches (Bennett, Desforges and Cockburn, 1981 and 1982).

It is, however, disconcerting for major pieces of research, such as Bennett's on 'teaching styles', to be published with a high profile (Bennett, 1976). The press has an over-simplified idea of teaching, learning and student achievements; they were only too ready to use the research to criticize the work of teachers in more open class-rooms. Criticism of the clustering techniques used to define the two broad categories of teachers led eventually to a re-working of the statistical data. Aitkin's interpretations received less publicity than Bennett's original, and in the public's mind there has probably been little shift in their general belief that formal education means better education (Aitkin, Bennett and Hesketh, 1981). From a teacher's point of view Aitkin's inclusion of variables which allow for variation between teachers within teaching styles is a major improvement.

The confidence of teachers in scientific research methods, applied to education, would be enhanced if researchers brought more precision to their work in establishing categories and selecting and observing variables. It would also be helpful if researchers were more tentative about their findings particularly when they know they are operating in sensitive areas of education. The very nature of research should produce a healthy scepticism which points to the problem of developing predictive educational theory using methods developed in the physical sciences.

One of the most influential pieces of research on the work of teachers has been the Rutter Report: *Fifteen Thousand Hours* (Rutter *et al.*, 1979). Its findings were attractive because they supported the idea that school can make a difference to a child's chances as a student. Criticism of the Report, from within the research community, often seemed to be esoteric point-scoring and produced a robust response from the Rutter team (Tizard *et al.*, 1980). Within the scope of their research programme they produced interesting correlations which were immediately embraced into the working life of many schools. If, however, you were a teacher concerned with, for example, the effect of public examinations on the school curriculum you were bound to see the Report as essentially conservative in character. Criticism of the Report for not looking radically at the chosen school outcomes failed to recognize the internal consistency of the research; there was no mystery about what was being researched. There will almost always remain some unease with large scale research of this kind. Methodology will be scrutinized, conclusions will be questioned, but above all there will be the lingering feeling that the research is too distanced from the work of practitioners and too little concerned with questioning the value of the subjects being researched.

Attempts to involve teachers in quantitative research have not met with much success. Cope and Gray argue that if teachers are to be involved in public debate and in the arena where decisions are taken on policy and resources, then members of their profession need to be conversant with research techniques (Cope and Gray, 1979).

Teachers operating within their unions, on examination panels, on schools-industry liaison boards and on LEA working parties, are all within the public arena where knowledge of research techniques and findings would be an advantage. In an ideal world there would be a member of staff in each school who, through in-service training or study experience, is able to comprehend that latest research and lead staff dialogue on the subject.

In arguing that there is a need for teachers to work with this type of research I would like to emphasize that I believe it is the responsibility of the researchers to make their work more comprehensible to teachers. Far too often teachers are presented with only the research findings which they feel obliged to accept or reject. Dialogue is discouraged by the use of specialist language which makes sense only to members of the research community. Finally the completion of a piece of research is too frequently seen as the end of the work; dissemination is a low priority with the result that teachers are inevitably discouraged from participating.

On Being Researched

At this point I would like to recall what it is like for a teacher to be part of the subject being researched. It follows naturally on from the feeling that researchers give insufficient thought to how to help teachers understand the nature and outcomes of research.

Teaching in an innovating large comprehensive school in the late 1960s was an exciting experience as teams of teachers developed courses designed to meet the needs of the whole ability range. It was the period immediately before ROSLA, when comprehensive schools were beginning to realize that being comprehensive was more than simply putting grammar and secondary modern schools together in the interest of the more efficient movement of children through the system.

We had regular requests from MA and PhD students to undertake research into our work. Two requests were accepted, one concerned with curriculum and learning, and the other with aspects of school management. At the end of the year we felt rather as though we had been used. In the first place one of the researchers dropped out after one term and handed over her findings to the other researcher without any discussion with the staff. During the course of the curriculum research, which involved detailed classroom observation, discussions between staff and the researcher were kept to a minimum. On completion of the research a slightly embarrassed researcher attempted to explain her conclusion to a bewildered group of teachers. It appeared they had, through their new course, been unconsciously inhibiting children's learning through the use of socially determined categories of knowledge. Scant regard was given to the fact that the course was an honest attempt to understand what might be meant by a common curriculum, and to the fact that, as a new integrated course, a number of staff were handling social science concepts for the first time. It was difficult to escape the feeling that the researcher had a very clear preconceived notion of how learning takes place, or doesn't take place in classrooms, and our innovation was being used to provide evidence to confirm her already fixed ideas. It was not long before we began to question why the researcher failed to see that her own research was an even more acute form of academic mystification than that engaged in by the teachers under scrutiny.

Probably the most damaging omission from the research was the failure to explain adequately the contexts within which the innovation was operating (this would ideally have covered national, LEA and school contexts). Teachers are generally very aware of the constraints on their work; the fact that the school, for example, placed an emphasis on instruction in most lessons made the introduction of enquiry work particularly difficult.

This particular series of experiences may not be typical of teachers' experience of being researched but they do provide an insight into the reasons why researchers need to be sensitive to how teachers perceive their work. It was some time after the completion of the research before the teachers could extract from the findings elements which were immediately helpful to their work in the classroom.

The Teacher as Researcher

One of the principal legacies of the curriculum movement in the 1960s and early 1970s was the idea that teachers could be involved in researching into learning in their own classrooms. Attempting to come to terms with the whole ability range in the one school emphasized critical questions about the knowledge and skills which should be represented in the curriculum. The teaching profession was far from united in understanding what the curriculum should provide in common for all students; ROSLA highlighted these differences of opinion. Some schools responded to the prospect of teaching sixteen year olds by devizing special courses which claimed to be practical, relevant and totally separate from the mainstream school commitment to examinations. Those schools who attempted, through the medium of mode III OL and CSE Examinations to devize common courses, developed through the integration of subjects, were saying that there is knowledge all students have a right to study.

Resolving questions of curriculum content ultimately rests on the values we seek to give expression to in the organization of schools. While we may turn to research for answers to some educational questions, reflection by philosophers such as John White was particularly relevant to those who felt that it was wrong for comprehensive schools to replicate the divisiveness of the grammar/secondary schools split. While the philosophers were making the case for all students to have access to the 'logical' divisions of knowledge, a branch of sociology was arguing that students' commonsense knowledge was the principal way they made sense of the world. This argument was related particularly to the learning of working class children which the sociologists saw as being inhibited by learning organized around the structures of disciplines. This latter perspective temporarily immobilized the thinking of some teachers.

Teachers were being encouraged to innovate, with the support of curriculum projects sponsored by the Schools Council, and to make sense of conflicting views being expressed by educationists operating in higher education. As the head of a faculty in a large comprehensive school at that time, I was helped in coming to terms with these conflicts by two particular projects. Jerome Bruner's research as a psychologist had particularly focused on children's concept attainment (Bruner, 1977). He received wide publicity for claiming that any subject can be taught in an intellectually honest way to any child. This assumes that learning can be structured in such a way that children are given access to the facts, concepts and validation processes which make up a subject. Bruner's researches were paralleled by a piece of curriculum development which attempted to introduce children to the concepts and inductive enquiry of the social sciences through a course which used anthropological materials as the principal evidence to be handled by children. 'Man: A course of study' was structured as a spiral curriculum with concepts being revisited throughout the course. The fact that the course was criticized for inhibiting children's feelings in the search for intellectual understanding, should not detract from the fact that Bruner was a university researcher working with teachers in a common concern with expanding our understanding of how children learn. The influence of the course went beyond the social studies department; it stimulated questions which transcended department boundaries. The analysis of subject structures, the organization of enquiry work and the induction of teachers into new ways of working have a general relevance to any school or department concerned with innovation.

Schools participating in the course had to go through an induction at the Centre for Applied Research in Education at the University of East Anglia. The fact that Lawrence Stenhouse set up this centre is not a coincidence as far as I am concerned. His work on the Humanities Curriculum Project was the second main influence on my own thinking. His original brief was to set up a curriculum project covering the Humanities which would help schools meet the demands of ROSLA. Early on in the Project's development he made two uncompromising decisions; one was to give emphasis to discussion as the principal learning experience, and the other was to use original documents as the stimulus for discussion. He was thus clearly stating that young people staying on in school should have the opportunity to discuss serious issues in an informed and serious way. The depth of thought given to helping teachers to understand their role in discussion, and to understanding the rationale of the whole project has left a legacy of knowledge and materials which must make the boundary between it being a curriculum project, as opposed to a research project, a very fine line.

The idea that teachers could improve their understanding of the education process by reflecting and researching into their own classroom practices grew out of his experience with the Humanities Curriculum Project. The problems associated with disseminating the project served to emphasize the importance of teachers developing the knowledge and skills which would enable them to carry out their own research and manage their own innovations.

Malcolm Skilbeck writing about Stenhouse's research methodology says:

> 'Central to Stenhouse's view of Education is the teacher, not the pupil, the school, the providing authorities or the policy makers. It is the teacher, purposive and free, informed by knowledge and understanding, with clearly articulated values, and a repertoire of practical skills, that he saw as the central agent in the educational enterprise and the ultimate focus of his views on research'. (Skilbeck, 1983)

To Stenhouse, teachers involved in research are not only developing their skills as professionals, but they are making explicit the problematic nature of the knowledge and processes they are responsible for organizing in their classrooms. (He shared with Bruner a strong resistance to the behavioural model of learning because it fails to take account of free human action.) They will be concerned with analyzing practical action through the systematic collection of data, analysis of data and its representation. Each teacher is involved in a unique piece of research which Stenhouse saw as possibly developing into a case study. These case studies would then be available to teachers and researchers in higher education to assist in the development and testing of hypotheses and to suggest new research priorities. Stenhouse placed great emphasis on the idea of the teacher as researcher making possible a partnership between practising teachers and lecturers in higher education, whose work is more theory based.

One of the principal problems of teachers undertaking research into their own classroom is how to move from analysis of what is taken for granted knowledge, and of intuitive teacher behaviour, into consideration of alternative ways of working. John Elliott describes this as moving from tacit professional knowledge to conscious reflection and investigation (Elliott, 1983). We need to resolve how this move is achieved if research by teachers is genuinely to extend their understanding of educational processes. Testing hypotheses developed in previous classroom researches, dialogue with professionals engaged in research and working in collaboration with colleagues who observe and record classroom behaviour, are all ways in which teachers may be able to take their research beyond consideration of the familiar. The ORACLE project (Observational Research and Classroom Learning Evaluation) illustrates how a University Institute of Education can work in partnership with teachers (Galton, 1983). It focuses on aspects of a teacher's classroom organization which appear as crucial factors in influencing what teachers and pupils do and say to each other during the course of a lesson. In describing their findings the researchers place great emphasis on a form of presentation with which teachers can identify. This then provides the teachers involved in ORACLE with concepts and categories around which to build their own research observations.

Despite the progress made in relating INSET to teacher-based research we are still a long way from there being a general agreement about the importance of teachers as researchers, and not surprisingly no significant body of research expertise has been built up in the profession. Experience of innovation, and the opportunity to reflect on schools from the outside, is the rare combination of experience which was no doubt partly responsible for Michael Armstrong carrying out a seminal piece of classroom research (Armstrong, 1980). His belief in the capacity of children to learn and understand for themselves, coupled with the detailed close observation of children produced insights which are at one and the same time both sensitive and powerful.

This quote from his final chapter illustrates why teachers who acknowledge that they are learning alongside the children, have much to contribute to the way our understanding of children's learning is improved.

> The study of play thus brings us back to the central theme of this book. How are we to understand the understanding of children? One way of beginning is to examine with careful sympathy, the thought and action of the children whom we ourselves are teaching. . . . I believe that a satisfactory theory of the life of reason from the beginnings of learning requires many examinations of this kind, alongside the work of other students of human development; psychologists, philosophers, sociologists, historians. In describing the intellectual life of a class of eight and nine year old children I have sought to draw attention to one particular feature of the early life of reason which seems to me to be of special consequence for the course of intellectual growth. That feature is the seriousness of purpose in children's thought and action: their high intent. We can observe it in their early writings, their art, their mathematics and their play: in every activity which absorbs them intellectually and emotionally. It is the quality of mind which acquires knowledge by appropriating knowledge. It is this seriousness of purpose that makes children's practice a significant performance rather than a course of training; it is this that justifies us in ascribing to children a creative and critical imagination. Ultimately, it is the quality of seriousness that permits us to describe the life of reason as beginning at, or close to, the beginnings of learning.

The enhancement of the professional skills and status of teachers can be linked to the development of research skills. The expansion of in-school evaluation builds on these skills and has also a particular relevance to professional development. If teacher training responds to HMI recommendations for teachers' involvement in training, and for partnership between schools and training institutes, then there will be the possibility of a closer link between teachers' research and that conducted from centres of higher education. The partnership will involve schools sharing in the training of teachers, and training institutes considering issues which are part of the daily concern of teachers.

Research by the LEAs and the DES

Schools often feel under pressure from research which involves statistical returns. Working in inner London I have rarely doubted the importance and value which teachers should attach to information based on the analysis of statistics. The criteria on which financial and other resources are allocated depend for their definition principally on the collection of relevant statistics. In the ILEA current policy initiatives covering improvements in the education of ethnic minorities, of girls and of working class children, have all developed from reports drawn up by Research and Statistics Branch. These reports not only cover the statistical evidence, but include commentary based on literature covering the areas of concern. They have the virtue of being written in language which makes the reports accessible to teachers.

Another aspect of working with the ILEA Research and Statistics Branch involved asking for their assistance in monitoring a major innovation. As a newly established comprehensive school we decided to introduce mixed ability teaching into all subjects in the first year. The fact that all subjects were involved, and therefore most departments and most teachers, we felt was worth monitoring. (So often schools only introduce mixed ability teaching in a minority of subjects.) The research investigated how the school arrived at the decision to introduce new groupings for children; children were tested in language and mathematics; teachers filled in attitude and behaviour scales and teachers filled in questionnaires on teaching mixed ability groups. It was our original intention as staff that the Authority might find useful information which might help other schools. In general we had the feeling that the autonomy of schools inhibited the exchange of information, both positive and negative, which might make a constructive contribution to developments in other schools. On reflection the real classroom problems we faced with mixed ability teaching would far more appropriately have been researched by teachers working in collaboration with colleagues documenting and building up case study material which as near as possible described what actually happened. (In 1974 we defined research exclusively in terms of an external researcher collecting data!) Case study material would have been complementary to the research data. This type of cooperation between an LEA and an individual school is unusual but worthy of serious consideration as a means of generating local data which may have general application within the LEA. Schools share many more features in common than they often choose to admit.

Research by the DES aimed at monitoring children has had little impact on the work of teachers. This can partly be attributed to the reports making few concessions to the average teacher's lack of knowledge about assessment procedures. Concern about the possible use of the APU tests to control the content of the curriculum, or to encourage teachers to teach to the tests, has so far proved unfounded. On the positive side APU tests in practical work, particularly science, have been able to extend our understanding of scientific achievement. There is, however, some evidence that LEAs might feel encouraged to extend their own testing procedures as part of their monitoring of standards. Some LEAs see criterion-referenced tests, covering basic aspects of learning, as the answer to the general problem of assessing children's progress. It is too early to say precisely how this would work but it is not too early to point to the potential generalizable tests of this kind can have, for narrowing the curriculum, and for focusing attention on a limited range of students' cognitive development. We should be aiming for more criterion-referenced assessment organized by teachers to widen the range of children's learning.

Research Priorities

In the present climate of education cuts it may seem presumptuous to be writing about priorities for future research in education. If we accept, however, that to work in education at any level should involve a commitment to learning by all participants then research is the *sine qua non* of a healthy education system. As an eclectic field of knowledge, education needs constant review and development as educationists refine its concepts, search for metaphors which illuminate processes and develop theories which almost certainly will be disproved. It is precisely because of the mood of uncertainty in education that we need to consider fresh ways of looking at old problems. The alternative is to retreat into defensive posturing which plays into the hands of traditionalists who operate with a degree of certainty about educational outcomes which is offensive to those concerned with the common rights and needs of all children.

Research ought to contribute to giving a sense of progress to those practitioners concerned with devizing and evaluating fresh approaches to comprehensive education. We perhaps are inclined sometimes to underestimate the contribution of the curriculum movement to classroom learning. Nevertheless, it should be a source of concern that our knowledge of why some innovations succeed and others fail does not seem to have produced lessons which influence current practice in any significant way. We know, for example, that innovations often fail because they are introduced into a context which is hostile and yet the idea of whole school policies on learning, judging by HMI reports, is far from being generally applied in schools. Perhaps the new management courses for headteachers will give emphasis to the head as senior professional (teacher). It is no longer sufficient for the headteacher to be senior executive exclusively; their involvement in the management of curriculum and learning will provide greater support for cross-curriculum issues and should enable research, whether by teachers or outsiders, to find a way into influencing the school's organization of learning. A closer partnership between schools and institutions of higher education is essential if we are to have a sense of development in our knowledge of schools, rather than a dependence on enthusiasm and individuals; the latter is a recipe for the continuation of our present faltering steps.

The professional development of teachers will be enhanced by such a partnership linked to teacher training and to the role of the teacher as researcher. We need to answer the question what constitutes the professional substantive knowledge of the teaching profession? We know demands on teachers have broadened but we have little idea of how it all adds up. Research is needed into the skills teachers require as researchers and into the conditions which facilitate their research; in the broad area of substantive knowledge we particularly need research into the knowledge teachers require to assess children's achievements and to evaluate their courses. The most effective way of resisting any attempts by the DES and the LEAs to influence curriculum content, through the imposition of testing procedures, is to demonstrate a thorough knowledge of assessment making a creative contribution to children's learning. Similarly, with evaluation, teachers need to know how to ground evaluation in the classroom experiences of children if the children's learning and the professional development of teachers are to benefit from the experience. Evaluation involving LEA checklists is less likely to reach into the significant experiences of children and to be more concerned with presenting as close a proximation to the model school, implied by the questionnaires, as the teachers can describe.

It is now fourteen years since the publication of *Language, the Learner and the School* by Douglas Barnes and James Britten (1969)

For many teachers this book represented a watershed in their understanding of how oral and written language relate to children's learning, and to their understanding of how certain policies on learning must permeate the whole school if they are to be effective. Recognizing that children are more likely to make new knowledge their own if they can first write and talk about it, in terms familiar to them, was a first step towards bridging the gap between the specialist received knowledge of disciplines, and the commonsense knowledge of children. At one time it looked as though research within the sociology of education might throw more light on our understanding of this problem. The work of M.F.D. Young certainly made many more people than were prepared to admit, in schools and higher education, more sensitive to the potential all disciplines have for mystifying students and falsifying how knowledge has developed.

Teachers today, particularly in the inner cities, are faced with children whose experiences range widely through youth subcultures, working and middle class communities and the cultures of ethnic minorities. How to respond to their rich variety of knowledge and expectations is a challenge to all teachers irrespective of their subject. Teachers as researchers may be ideally placed to observe how colleagues extend and develop children's knowledge gained through experience into a broader understanding of concepts and processes used by subjects. Research into how children make these links and how teachers can facilitate links would also benefit from contributions made by researchers in higher education. Current concerns with multicultural education and the education of girls need to be placed into this broader-based context of curriculum research. The tendency for them to be considered in isolation from more basic educational issues encourages LEAs to consider solutions through the work of experts. This approach to curriculum innovation is the antithesis of the idea that teachers can be researchers. Experts can only succeed if teachers are able to provide a supportive context within which they can work; otherwise we are back to the world of enthusiasts responding to experts and away from serious consideration of the professional development of teachers.

Denis Lawton speaking to the British Educational Research Association specified four priorities for research in the immediate future (Lawton, 1983).

1   The effects of cuts in a school over a period of years.
2   The unintended consequences of the Manpower Services Commission's intervention in schools by means of the

technical and vocational educational initiatives.

3   Case studies of successful examples of mixed ability teaching.

4   Case studies of successful mode III CSE examination work.

Mode III examinations and mixed ability teaching are associated with progressive developments in comprehensive education. Examples of good practice do need documenting in part because progress with these developments has been so piecemeal both between schools and more disturbingly within schools. The absence of a clear emerging rationale for comprehensive education also leads to confusion over school and LEA attitudes towards Government initiatives in technical and vocational education. It is now ten years since Pat Daunt argued for schools to embrace the central guiding principle that all students are of equal value. For many teachers this has been the criterion by which they have judged their school's developments and their own organization of classroom learning. In the present political and economic climate it is more than ever important that research should be seen to contribute to our understanding of the broad purposes of comprehensive education. We need constantly to be reminded that shared purpose in education comes from shared aims.

I would not like to leave the impression that all educational research should grow out of the immediate needs of schools. The fact that comprehensive education has been with us for so long, and yet still seems vulnerable to outside criticism, suggests that there is ample scope for the more detached researcher to push forward the frontiers of our thinking. Following the exacting research procedures required for academic acceptance is the most straightforward aspect of research; what we also need is the intuitive thinking which sees fresh questions which need answering. Working in education can be such an overwhelming experience that we fail to see beyond our immediate experience. At every level research should be helping us to question our assumptions and to move confidently to embrace alternative ways of working. It should be the basis for partnership between schools and institutions in higher education.

References

AITKIN, M.A., BENNETT, S.N. and HESKETH, J. (1981) 'Teaching Styles and Pupil Progress; a re-analysis', *British Journal of Educational Psychology*, 51, pp. 170–186.

ARMSTRONG, M. (1980) *Closely Observed Children*, London, Chameleon Books.

BARNES, D., BRITTEN, J. and ROSEN, H. (1969) *Language, the Learner, and the School*, Harmondsworth, Penguin.

BENNETT, S.N. (1976) *Teaching Styles and Pupil Progress*, London, Open Books.

BENNETT, S.N., DESFORGES, C.W. and COCKBURN, A. (1981 and 1982) *The Quality of Pupil Learning Experiences*, Interim Reports to the Social Science Research Council, London, SSRC.

BRUNER, J. *et al.* (1977) *A Study of Thinking*, New York, Wiley.

COPE, E. and GRAY, J. (1979) 'Teachers as researchers: some experience of an alternative paradigm', *British Educational Research Journal*, 5, 1, pp. 237–251.

ELLIOTT, J. (1983) 'Self-evaluation: professional development and accountability', in GALTON, M. and MOON, R. (Eds.) *Changing Schools ... Changing Curriculum*, London, Harper and Row, pp. 224–247.

GALTON, M. (1983) 'Classroom research and the teacher', in GALTON, M. and MOON, R. (Eds.) *Changing Schools ... Changing Curriculum*, London, Harper and Row, pp. 295–310.

LAWTON, D. (1983) 'The politics of educational research', *Times Educational Supplement*, 9 September 1983, p. 4.

RUTTER, M. *et al* (1979) *Fifteen Thousand Hours*, London, Open Books.

SKILBECK, M. (1983) 'Lawrence Stenhouse: research methodology', *British Educational Research Journal*, 9, 1, pp. 11–20.

TIZARD, B. *et al* (1980) *Fifteen Thousand Hours: A Discussion*, London, London Institute of Education, Bedford Way Papers.

An Analysis of an Individual's Educational Development: The Basis for Personally Oriented Action Research

Jack Whitehead

My purpose is to draw your attention to the development of a living form of educational theory. The theory is grounded in the lives of professional educators and their pupils and has the power to integrate within itself the traditional disciplines of education. Educational theory occupies an ambiguous position in the educational profession. Its importance is due to the fact that a profession supports its skills and techniques with a body of systematically produced theory. On the other hand, teachers tend to decry educational theory because of its lack of relationship to their practical skills and techniques.

My purpose in writing this chapter is to outline how I think a professionally credible educational theory could be generated and tested from a form of teacher action-research. I take teacher action-research to be a form of self-reflective inquiry undertaken by participants in educational contexts in order to improve the rationality and justice of:

(a)   their own educational practices,
(b)   their understanding of these practices,
(c)   the situations in which the practices are carried out.
      'It is most empowering when undertaken by participants collaboratively, though it is often undertaken by individuals sometimes in co-operation with "outsiders"' (Kemmis and Carr, 1983).

I am assuming that a teacher action-researcher, who is interested in contributing to knowledge of the process of improving education within schools, will be faced by an academic community who will examine the legitimacy of the claim to knowledge. I am also assuming that a teacher-researcher is concerned to establish a direct relationship between the claim to know what he or she is doing and the pupils' educational development.

The educational analysis which follows is focused upon the nature of the validity of an individual action-researcher's claim to know his or her own educational development. The analysis outlines a form of educational theory which can be generated from professional practice and which can integrate the different contributions of the disciplines of education. Let me say at the beginning how I see the relationship between my own research and teacher action-research. In my work in a university I am paid to make a scholarly and acknowledged contribution to knowledge of my subject, education. I characterize my attempts to make this contribution a form of academic action-research. In my investigations of my own claims to know my own educational development I have explored the nature of a form of educational theory which is directly related to educational practice. My particular concerns have focused upon the academic legitimacy of an individual's claim to know his or her own educational development. I think that my findings will be of use to those teacher-researchers who wish to justify their own claims to knowledge to the academic community.

The approach to educational theory I am suggesting we adopt rests on a number of assumptions concerning both the idea of a 'living form of theory' and the personal and social criteria which can be used to criticize the theory. I use the term a 'living form of theory' to distinguish the suggested approach from the 'linguistic form' in which traditional theories are presented for criticism. In a living approach to educational theory I am suggesting that teacher action-researchers present their claims to know how and why they are attempting to overcome practical educational problems in this form:

> I experience a problem when some of my educational values are negated in my practice.
> I imagine a solution to my problem.
> I act in the direction of the solution.
> I evaluate the outcomes of my actions.
> I modify my problems, ideas and actions in the light of my evaluations.

For educational theory to be directly related to educational practice it must have the power to explain an individual's development. One of the major problems which has led to the discrediting of traditional forms of educational theory was that they could not produce adequate explanations for the educational development of individuals. A theory should also be able to answer questions concerning why things happen. In the approach to educational theory advocated here the 'why' questions are answered in terms of 'value'. Like Ilyenkov (1982) I take 'value' to be a human goal for the sake of which we struggle to give our lives their particular form. In relation to the enquiry I take it that the experience of the negation of educational values moves the enquiry forward and that the values are taken, by the holder, to be concrete universal laws in the sense that we hold our educational values with universal intent.

Questions concerning the academic legitimacy of a claim to knowledge are often focused upon the criticism of a particular piece of work. The work being criticized can be a single hypothesis or theory (Popper 1972) or a research programme (Lakatos 1972). Whatever is being criticized is known as the unit of appraisal. In criticizing a claim to knowledge it is important to be clear about the unit and the standards of judgment which can legitimately be used in the criticism. There is some dispute amongst philosophers about the nature of the standards which can be used to criticize a claim to knowledge.

The unit of appraisal in my conception of educational theory is the individual's claim to know his or her own educational development. Although this unit may appear strange to most educational researchers I think that it is clearly comprehensible. The standards of judgment are however more difficult to communicate. I use both personal and social standards in justifying my own claims to know my own educational development. In using personal criteria I draw upon the work of Michael Polanyi. I am grateful for *Personal Knowledge* (1958) because in my case Polanyi fulfilled his purpose of 'stripping away the crippling mutilations which centuries of objectivist thought have imposed on the minds of men'. The personal criteria I use in making a claim to know my own educational development include Polanyi's values of respect and commitment.

> To claim validity for a statement merely declares that it ought to be accepted by everyone because everyone ought to be able to see it ... The affirmation of a scientific truth has an obligatory character; in this it is like all other valuations that are declared universal by our own respect for them. (Polanyi and Prosch, 1975)

> It is the act of commitment in its full structure that saves personal knowledge from being merely subjective. Intellectual commitment is a responsible decision, in submission to the compelling claims of what in good conscience I conceive to be true. It is an act of hope, striving to fulfil an obligation within a personal situation for which I am not responsible and which therefore determines my calling. This hope and this obligation are expressed in the universal intent of personal knowledge.
>
> ... Any conclusion, whether given as a surmise or claimed as a certainty, represents a commitment of the person who arrives at it. No one can utter more than a responsible commitment of his own, and this completely fulfils his responsibility for finding the truth and telling it. Whether or not it is the truth can be hazarded only by another, equally responsible commitment. (Polanyi, 1958.)

In grounding my epistemology in *Personal Knowledge* I am conscious that I have taken a decision to understand the world from my own point of view, as a person claiming originality and exercising his personal judgment responsibly with universal intent. This commitment determines the nature of the unit of appraisal in my claim to knowledge. The unit is the individual's claim to know his or her own educational development.

The social criteria I use to criticize my claim to knowledge appear to conform to Habermas' view on what claims to validity I am making if I wish to participate in a process of reaching understanding with you. Habermas (1979) says that I must choose a comprehensible expression so that we can understand one another. I must have the intention of communicating a true proposition so that we can share my claim to knowledge. I must want to express my intentions truthfully so that we can believe what I say. Finally, I must choose an utterance that is right so that we can accept what I say and we can agree with one another with respect to a recognized normative background. Moreover, communicative action can continue undisturbed only as long as participants suppose that the validity claims they reciprocally raise are justified.

From this I take it that the action-researcher has a responsibility to present a claim to knowledge for public criticism in a way which is comprehensible. The researcher must justify the propositional content of what he or she asserts, and justify the values which are used to give a form to the researcher's life in education. The researcher must be authentic in the sense of wanting to express his intentions truthfully. Habermas says, and I agree, that a claim to authenticity can only be realized in interaction: 'in the interaction it will be shown in time, whether the other side is "in truth or honestly" participating or is only pretending to engage in communicative action'.

The personal and social standards I use to judge the academic legitimacy of my claim to knowledge are the values I use in giving my life its particular form in education. In judging my own claim to educational knowledge I use the following logical, scientific, ethical and aesthetic values. In such a brief space all I can hope to do is to sketch out the general principles of my position and to draw your attention to the locations where the position is being worked out in more detail in practice. The most difficult problem to be overcome in presenting my ideas to others in a comprehensible way concerns the logic of my position. As a dialectician I am aware of the attacks on dialectical logic by such eminent Western philosophers as Karl Popper. Popper (1963) dismisses the use of dialectical logic in the presentation of theories as based on nothing better than a loose and woolly way of speaking. His case rests on the way he thinks about contradictions. The point at issue has been clearly put by Ilyenkov (1977).

> Contradiction as the concrete unity of mutually exclusive opposites is the real nucleus of dialectics, its central category ... but no small difficulty immediately arises as soon as matters touch on 'subjective dialectics', on dialectics as the logic of thinking. If any object is a living contradiction, what must the thought (statement about the object) be that expresses it? Can and should an objective contradiction find reflection in thought? And if so, in what form?

Formal logicians such as Popper (1963) hold that any theory which contains contradictions is entirely useless as a theory. This view is based upon a linguistic presentation of theory. In this paper I am drawing your attention to the locations (Note 1) where a living form of educational theory is being produced. The theory is embodied in the lives of practitioners who exist as living contradictions. The inclusion of 'I' as a living contradiction within a theoretical presentation creates problems if we attempt this presentation in a purely propositional form because the propositional logic holds that we cannot have two mutually exclusive statements which are true simultaneously.

In my own development I am conscious of attempting to overcome the experience of myself as a living contradiction in order to minimize the tensions between, for example, values negated in practice and the current practice. I am also conscious of the need to give a form to my life and of the need for meaning and purpose. If I attempt to describe my development in a purely propositional form I will fail to communicate my meaning because of the existence of 'I' as a living contradiction in my development. The central problem is how to present a dialectical claim to knowledge in a publicly criticizable form. My own presentation is in the form of ten research reports (Whitehead 1982) produced over the past ten years as I have explored my existence in terms of 'I' as a living contradiction in the School of Education of the University of Bath. The table in Appendix 1 summarizes the educational analysis of my educational development. I would also draw your attention to the work of colleagues and students of mine, past and present, who are struggling in a similar way to improve the quality of education (see Note 2). By drawing your attention to where the theory is being generated and tested in practice, I hope to emphasize that it is embodied in the form of life of practitioners rather than existing in a propositional form within textbooks on library shelves.

This is not to deny that the propositional form can have significance for the genesis of educational theory. On the contrary the standards I use to justify my claim to know my own development as a scientific form of life are drawn from Popper's (1972) views on the logic of scientific discovery. The main difference between the traditional view of educational theory and the dialectical approach is that the traditional view was presented in a propositional form which excluded dialectical logic. The dialectical approach is presented in terms of the forms of life of individuals in education and shows how propositional forms exist within the forms of life.

In using Popper's work I check to see whether or not the claim to know my own educational development conforms to the cycle of experiencing and formulating problems, imagining a solution, acting on the imagined solution, evaluating the outcomes and modifying the problems and ideas. This capacity of the dialectical approach to integrate within itself the insights from a propositional form is what gives the approach its power to integrate the concepts of the disciplines of education. I think that this power rests upon the imaginative capacity of individuals to relate the concepts to their practical concerns. For example as the individual encounters personal and social constraints in his or her attempts to improve the quality of education in schools, the concepts from the psychology or sociology of education might prove useful in helping to overcome the barriers to improvement. The form I suggested above for the presentation of our claims to know our own educational development has the capacity to allow the inclusions of the concepts from the disciplines of education whilst being itself irreducible to the form of any of the present disciplines of education.

As the individual presents a claim to educational knowledge the academic community will be able to judge whether or not the work demonstrates an understanding of contemporary accounts in the different disciplines of education. It might also be the case that the claims to educational knowledge could point out deficiences in the present state of development of the disciplines of education.

Because of a desire to give a correct account of the nature of educational theory I want to hold up the value-laden nature of my claim to knowledge for public criticism. I want you to understand and accept for good reasons, the normative background of my ethical values.

I recognize a major problem, almost as great as the problem of contradiction, as soon as I attempt to communicate the ethical values in my claim to know my educational development. The problem is grounded in the principle known as the autonomy of ethics. This principle, usually attributed to Hume (1738) and upheld by linguistic philosophers, holds that statements of value and statements of fact form logically independent realms of discourse. In my educational development matters of fact and matters of value are integrated in my experience of practical problems of the kind, 'How do I improve this process of education here?'. How then do I present a claim to know my educational development in a way that truly represents this integration?

I can talk about the ethical values I use in making decisions which give a form to my life in education. I can use value-words such as those of consideration of interest, worthwhile activities, respect for persons and democratic forms of social control (Peters 1966). The meanings of my ethical values are however embodied in my educational practice. Their meanings emerge in the course of my attempts to overcome their negation (Feyerabend, 1975). In order to communicate these meanings I think that it is necessary to present visual records of that practice. I must show you where I am experiencing the denial of my educational values, give a public formulation of my problems in terms of the denial and I must present a programme of activities which I believe will overcome the denial. I must show you my actions and hold up my evaluations of those actions for your criticism. In this way it is possible for an individual to hold up a claim to know his or her educational development as an ethical form of life for public scrutiny. The individual can thus generate a personal form of educational theory and submit it for public test.

However, since the meaning of values cannot be expressed in a purely linguistic form of discourse, they must, as I have said, be shown in action. Hence, it will be necessary for whoever is validating the claim to knowledge to use ostensive, as well as linguistic, criticism, in judging this aspect of the claim to knowledge. In judging the legitimacy of a value-laden claim to knowledge the individual is faced with the problem of justifying one set of values against another. In recent Islamic publications (Abdullah 1982), for example, the Western view of democracy has been declared inimical to educational theory viewed from an Islamic perspective. My own justification for my educational values is grounded within Polanyi's view of personal knowledge. Given that I am using a particular set of values in attempting to give my life its particular form in education, I am committed to examining the implications of attempting to overcome the experience of the negation of these values, in a way which fulfils Habermas' views on the validity claims I must fulfil if I am to reach an understanding with you. If our values conflict it seems to me inevitable that we are engaged in a political struggle. Conflict is most intensive when particular forms of life cut across those of others to the extent of one form negating the value-laden practice of another.

In the justification of a claim for scientific status for the individual's claim to know his or her own educational development I advocated the use of criteria from the work of Popper. To judge the logical status of the claim I suggested the use of a dialectical logic based on the work of Ilyenkov. To judge the ethical status I explained that my values were embodied in practice and that public criticism of the ethical base of my claim would require a form of ostensive criticism in which I must present visual records of my practice. I recognize that the cultural relativity of ethical values presents a serious problem for educators in a multicultural society who are asked to justify their own educational values. How the problem is being resolved must be shown and criticized in practice.

The final criterion is concerned with the notion of authenticity. This is a difficult concept to define because I think of education as a form of art in the sense that the individual is attempting to give a form to his or her life in a way which does not violate the integrity of other individuals. The aesthetic standard I use in judging the authenticity of the claim to knowledge requires an approach I have termed, following Holbrook (1979), 'indwelling'. Its use involves an ability on the part of the reader to empathize (through written, aural and visual records) with another individual's form of life as it is presented in a claim to knowledge and, through 'delicate intuitions, imagination and respect' (Russell, 1916), to judge whether or not the form of life can be seen in terms of the quality of human relationships in which the unity of humanity appears to be possible.

Just as the artist attempts to give a form to his or her material, so teachers, who are practizing the art of education, are giving a form to their own lives in education and assisting their pupils to do the same. When the artist presents his or her work, the appreciation of it will come as the viewer spends time 'reliving the work of its creator' (Lipps in Holbrook, 1979). In a similar way, in judging the aesthetic form of a claim to know another individual's form of life in education, the reader must attempt to identify with the process in which that individual struggled to give a form to his or her life in education. In affirming or rejecting the claim to knowledge as embodying an aesthetic form of life it is necessary, I think, for the reader to judge whether the quality of the actions presented in the claim to knowledge has violated the integrity of an individual or the unity of humanity as a whole. I say this because education has, for me, significance not only for its personal influence but also for its role in the world as a whole.

In offering the unit of appraisal and the standards of judgment which I think can be used by educational action-researchers to establish the academic legitimacy of their claims to knowledge I wish to emphasize that the logic of education proposed by Hirst and Peters (1970) is mistaken: ' . . . facts are only relevant to practical decisions about educational matters in so far as they are made relevant by some general view of what we are about when we are educating people. It is the purpose of this book to show the ways in which a view of education must impose such a structure on our practical decisions.'

In my view of educational theory the theory is essentially transformatory. Structures may exist in the process of transformation but they must not be *imposed* on the individual. The idea of imposing a structure is inconsistent with the view of educational knowledge proposed above. I would remind readers that they should always bear Polanyi's point in mind and approach their own claims to knowledge in a creative and critical way as individuals who have made a decision to understand the world from their own point of view, and who are claiming originality and exercising their judgments with universal intent. For the sake of the development of the profession of education they should also feel obliged to offer their claims to knowledge in an open forum for rational criticism.

Every educational action-researcher has a part to play in the development of the profession. Teacher action-researchers must be prepared to make public the educational theory which is embodied in their practices. Academic action-researchers must be prepared to help to establish the standards of judgment which are appropriate for judging the validity of such claims to knowledge. Administrator action-researchers must be prepared to show in what sense their activities are sustaining or improving the quality of education with the pupils in their institutions. My own work is concerned with assisting teacher action-researchers to justify their professional claims to know what they are doing through the provision of standards of judgment which themselves can stand the test of public and rational criticism. The only reason I have for writing this Chapter is the hope that it will lead you to contact some of those action-researchers who are participating in the programme or who are described in the bibliography and notes. Through such contact we hope that a shared form of educational theory will be generated and tested in our professional practices. We believe that this will lead to improvement in the quality of education in our educational and other social institutions.

Notes

1 *The Need for a Conference*
The past five years have seen an upsurge in the potential of action research as a way of relating practical and theoretical work in education, and thereby improving the quality of classroom learning. A number of our higher degree students have submitted dissertations using an action research approach and an increasing number of students are registering with us because of the work we do in this area. Because of the work either completed or in progress we are now able to organize a one-day conference which we hope will bring teachers, academics and administrators together. We hope to develop a network of action researchers and also to contribute to in-service days and to DES courses which could help teachers to explore the nature of their educational practice.

2 The ideas in this Chapter have developed over a number of years through the collaboration, criticism and support of colleagues and students. In particular I have benefited from the support of Dr. Cyril Selmes and Mary Tasker in the School of Education at the University of Bath and from the unpublished Masters Degree dissertations, listed below, of students who

have worked with me to improve the quality of education in both theory and practice.

BARRETT, M. (1982) 'An approach to the in-service professional development of teachers', University of Bath.

FORREST, M. (1983) 'The teacher as researcher — the use of historical artefacts in primary schools', University of Bath.

FOSTER, D. (1982) 'Explanations for teachers' attempts to improve the quality of education for their pupils', University of Bath.

GREEN, B. (1979) 'Personal dialectics in educational theory and educational research methodology', University of London.

HAYES, G. (1980) 'An investigation of educational practice in the classroom', University of Bath.

PETERS, C. (1980) 'Research into the evaluation of youth work', University of Bath.

References

ABDULLAH, M. (1982) *Educational Theory: A Koranic Perspective*, Saudi Arabia, Umm Al-Qura University.

FEYERABEND, P. (1975) *Against Method*, London, Verso.

HABERMAS, J. (1979) *Communication and the Evolution of Society*, London, Heinemann.

HIRST, P. and PETERS, R.S. (1970) *The Logic of Education*, London, Routledge and Kegan Paul.

HOLBROOK, D. (1980) *What It Means To Be Human*, unpublished manuscript, Cambridge, Kings College.

HUME, D. (1738) *Treatise on Human Nature*, Oxford, Oxford University Press.

ILYENKOV, E. (1982) *The Dialectic of the Abstract and the Concrete in Marx's Capital*, Moscow, Progress Publishers.

ILYENKOV, E. (1977) *Dialectical Logic*, Moscow, Progress Publishers.

KEMMIS, S. and CARR, W. (1983) *Becoming Critical — Knowing Through Action Research*, Deakin, Deakin University Press.

KOSOK, (1976) 'The systematization of dialectical logic for the study of development and change', in *Human Development*, 19, pp. 325–350.

MEDAWAR, P. (1969) *Induction and Intuition in Scientific Thought*, London Methuen.

MITROFF, I. and KILMAN, R. (1978) *Methodological Approaches To Social Science*, San Francisco, Jossey-Bass.

PETERS, R.S. (1966) *Ethics and Education*, London, Allen and Unwin.

POLANYI, M. (1958) *Personal Knowledge*, London, Routledge and Kegan Paul.

POLANYI, M. and PROSCH, H. (1975) *Meaning*, Chicago, University of Chicago Press.

POPPER, K. (1963) *Conjectures and Refutations*, London, Routledge and Kegan Paul.

WHITEHEAD, A.J. (1982) 'Assessing and evaluating an individual's educational development', *Assessment and Evaluation in Higher Education*, 7, 1, pp. 22–47.

Appendix 1

The Form of Life of a Living Contradiction

Report	1	2	3	4	5	6	7	8	9/10
Medawar's phase of scientific enquiry	critical	creative	critical	creative	critical	creative	critical	creative	critical
The Popperian schema	s_1	—	s_2	—	s_3	—	s_4	—	s_5
Mitroff's and Kilman's methodological approach	analytic scientist	—	conceptual theorist	—	conceptual humanist	—	particular humanist	—	—
Kosok's self-linearizing form	A non-linear dialectic process depicted as a self-linearizing form which reveals transition structures (in the schemas and critical phases) as nodal points of self-reflection								

Ensuring Practical Outcomes from Educational Research

Neville Bennett and Charles Desforges

The golden age of educational research came to an end sixty years ago. As Travers (1983) records, 'the first quarter of the present century was an age of enthusiasm for educational research, and a productive one. But educational research could not possibly be as productive as the enthusiasts in the schools expected it to be. It could not live up to expectations. The result was a later disillusionment among school administrators ... that has lingered on until the present day.' The sentiment of this latter statement is reflected in Yates' (1971) pessimistic summary of the relationship between researchers and practitioners in which he maintained that it was characterized by misunderstanding and recrimination. Policy makers, administrators and teachers criticized researchers for pursuing esoterica instead of tackling day-to-day problems, and even when the odd report was seen as marginally relevant it was so couched in jargon that it only served 'to camouflage glimpses of the obvious'. Researchers in turn criticized teachers for blindly following the latest bandwagon, and for holding misconceptions of the researcher's role.

Ensuring practical outcomes of research, even when that was a primary objective of the study, was not likely to occur in such a climate. Fortunately the research community has reacted over the last decade both to generate a more positive climate and to initiate approaches toward the implementation of research findings in classrooms and schools. The first part of this chapter summarizes these efforts prior to a consideration of what educational research might aspire to as an applied science.

Approaches to Ensuring Practical Outcomes

1 Dissemination

The first hurdle to be overcome was the oft-quoted communication gap. In his report of the 1967 UNESCO conference Yates (1971) referred to the fact that 'one of the major obstacles to the effective dissemination of research results is the stubborn fact that those to whom information is addressed are unwilling to give it their full attention'. This assumed of course that researchers had something worthwhile to say. Nevertheless lack of communication was a central finding of the study by Cane and Schroeder (1971) and by Hounsell *et al* (1980) a decade later. Pleas for more effective communication increased, typical being the rallying cry of Burdin (1976), 'It's time to get research reports off the shelf and into the hands of those responsible for education who can apply them. Until we do educational research too often will remain an exercise in futility'. Despite the huge oversimplification of such rhetoric the purveyors of research funding were, by the mid-seventies, making the same claim. Wrigley (1977), then Chairman of the Educational Research Board of SSRC, called for bolder approaches from researchers who should be prepared to take more risks, and for publications to achieve maximum effect on the various audiences. And Kay (1977), then Head of DES Research, concluded that 'the publicity that may follow such wider dissemination of research findings carries risks since it often distorts in an attempt to simplify. Nevertheless the risks must be taken if the general public is either to recognize the potential importance of educational research, or to be influenced by it'. The problems of writing for multiple audiences are outlined elsewhere (Bennett 1978), nevertheless the trend for researchers to target their research reports at teachers and teacher educators rather than at their academic peers is a significant development (*cf.* Galton *et al*, 1980; Bennett *et al*, 1984). It is however still no more than an act of faith at this stage since there is yet no evidence that improved dissemination leads to greater changes in practice. On the other hand Nisbet (1980) may be correct in arguing that educational research is a mode of thinking rather than a shortcut to answers. 'In the long run the real influence of educational research is through its effect on the attitudes of those who teach.'

Few would disagree that effective dissemination is to be encouraged but many would admit that such indirect methods of influencing practice have far less impact than actually involving teachers in research. Influencing teaching through direct involvement takes many forms, and two distinct approaches are now considered, one in which teachers are passive and manipulated and the other in which they are active and collaborative.

2 *Experimental Intervention Programmes*

Experimental interventions into teaching are increasing as researchers attempt to implement their findings. Two modes can be discerned, prescriptive and non-prescriptive, with the former being predominant. Indeed non-prescriptive interventions are rare. The most recent of these is by Bennett *et al* (1984) who designed an experimental in-service course as part of an SSRC project on classroom tasks (Bennett and Desforges, 1981). Here case studies were utilized to highlight issues in the classroom task process to stimulate discussion and analysis among groups of teachers prior to a skill-based element on teacher diagnosis of pupil misunderstandings. In this particular example the in-service course itself was used as a data base since transcripts of teacher discussions were used to refine understandings of teacher conceptualization.

Prescriptive intervention programmes use the same general approach:

1 Translate correlational findings into implications for teacher behaviour.
2 Develop training materials and procedures based on these implications.
3 Observation of teacher behaviour in the classroom environment before, during and after teacher training.
4 Measurement of pupil achievement and/or activities subsequent to their teaching by trained and control teachers.

Crawford and Stallings (1978) report such a study drawing on the process-product correlational research of Brophy and Evertson (1974) and Stallings and Kaskowitz (1974). Packets of materials were produced in the broad areas of behaviour management, general instructional methods and questioning and feedback techniques. Two experimental and one control group were used. The first experimental group received a training course on the materials; the second experimental group received only the materials and the control group received nothing.

The findings indicated that, if followed, the training materials hold out the likelihood that pupils will manifest increased engagement time on academic material and ultimately increase performance.

Somewhat surprisingly it was also found that the experimental group receiving training implemented the programme no better than those who simply received the materials. However a later study by Gage and Colardarci (1980) found few differences between a group of teachers who received only the material and a control group. They did however find that where teachers conformed to the materials these correlated with higher class achievement scores. Mackay (1979) and Good and Grouws (1979) found similar relationships in studies which followed this general approach. On the basis of their study Good and Grouws maintained that their data were an important contradiction to the frequently expressed attitudes that teaching is too complex to be approached scientifically and/or that these inexpensive treatments cannot hope to bring about significant results.

Finally two studies have utilized the same approach in the area of classroom environment. Emmer *et al* (1981) found that the pupils of teachers who implemented the programme showed a significantly higher level of task engagement and appropriate behaviour than those who did not. A current study on this issue is the IEA Classroom Environment study which is being undertaken on an international scale. Following a correlational study they too aim to create experimental programmes to determine the degree to which the recommended teaching practices are being fostered by the training programme and to what extent changes in practice contribute to improved student achievement and attitudes.

Although these empirically based intervention approaches do appear to succeed, at least partially, in implementing research findings in the classroom they are not immune from criticism. It has been argued, for example, that they place teachers in a passive role which diminishes their autonomy. The writings of Stenhouse (1975) epitomize this view. He argued that it is not sufficient that teachers' work be studied; teachers 'should study their own work', and that 'fruitful development in the field of curriculum and teaching depends upon evolving styles of cooperative research by teachers and using full time researchers to support the teachers' work'. 'Communication is less effective than community in the utilization of knowledge.' The view that schools should take responsibility for evaluating and monitoring themselves, particularly in the wake of pressures for accountability, has led to an increasing call for collaborative ventures between researchers and teachers.

3 Collaborative Research

The advantages of collaborative research with teachers are, according to Tikunoff and Ward (1983), threefold. Firstly the results are more likely to be used if the consumers are involved in the research process. Secondly, such involvement is more likely to lead to the complexities of classroom life being recognized, and thirdly, the time lapse between research and implementation will be markedly reduced. However all these advantages would seem to be dependent on the extent of teacher participation and the extent to which the research questions posed reflect teachers' concerns and priorities.

What form does collaborative research take? This is not a straightforward question to answer since the term is a generic one encompassing many types of cooperative endeavours, some specifically defined and others not. Tikunoff and Ward (1983) summarize a range of studies on different content areas, from disruptive behaviour to class size, and from the acquisition of writing literacy to a whole school inquiry on producing successful school outcomes. They draw on these to specify six characteristics of collaborative research.

1   That practitioners be involved in the research process when the outcomes are intended to inform their practice.
2   Study should focus on the concerns of practitioners.
3   Decision making should be collaborative throughout each stage of the inquiry.
4   Recognition that collaborative inquiry can provide professional growth for researchers as well as practitioners.
5   Attention should be paid not only to the research but also to the potential application of the findings.
6   The complexity of the classroom should be recognized whilst maintaining the integrity of the instructional activity.

However only one of the studies summarized met all these criteria. The participating teachers were most frequently utilized in the process of data analysis and in collecting part of the data set. In one half of the studies they were involved in formulating data collection procedures. In only a third were they involved in the formulation of the research question, and, as surprising, only a quarter used the teachers to implement the findings. If these studies are typical of collaborative efforts in the United States there is still some way to go before they could be considered as reactive to teachers' or school needs.

Experience in Britain also shows that the nature of collaborative endeavours varies markedly in membership, purpose and content. Bennett and O'Hare (1980) for example outlined several modes established at the University of Lancaster. When the scheme was first initiated in the mid-1970s teacher-research groups were established to carry out small scale studies under the guidance of a consultant. Although successful in stimulating interest in research such groups were overtaken by a combination of the pressures of accountability and the service offered gaining wider publicity in the region. As such the general approach changed from a teacher-centred mode initiated by the university to a school-based mode initiated by schools. As such the Centre is now reactive to a range of school-based issues, the methodological approach to which depends entirely on the problem posed.

In the last few years questions on curriculum and assessment have been in the majority and may emanate from a whole school, department(s) within a school or an individual teacher. In each case a consultant holds a preliminary discussion to secure a common agreement with senior school management which is then transformed into a written contract. Further discussions are then held, often with the whole staff, on the topic of concern in order to formulate and refine the research question(s). Data collection procedures are agreed before the staff gather the data. In all cases the Centre provides help with data analysis when required before being interpreted by staff members.

The role of consultant is crucial, in helping staff to frame their ideas more coherently, stimulating awareness of alternatives and the implications of differing research procedures. This can be a full-time member of the university staff or an experienced teacher following the MA programme.

Not only does this approach allow practical outcomes to be implemented quickly, it also ensures coherent links between theory and practice for the teacher-consultant concerned. This same link is used by Elliott (1980) in developing a diploma course around school-based research, and in a different form by Gagne (1980). Gagne's view is that the best way to bring about acceptance of research by teachers is to involve them in the research process, and that such research should be decision-oriented, small scale, and guided by agencies which have the research expertise and well established links with schools. He reports training three members of staff of each of twenty-seven primary schools who then acted as consultants in their school in such activities as working with staff in problem definition and relevant methodology.

Collaborative research thus takes many forms. Their purposes are similar but there is no clear consensus regarding the interlinked issues of the teacher's role in such endeavours and the methodology to be employed.

In some centres, such as that at Lancaster, the problem clearly defines the method, a view endorsed by Nixon (1979). He firmly concluded that teachers should participate in classroom research by initiating inquiry or collaborating in inquiries originating within the school or from outside agencies. He sees the role of collaboration as enhancing professional self-development, improving practice and developing pedagogy. As such, research and teaching should be seen as interdependent, each activity informing the other and ultimately improving the quality of education in the classroom. He argued against accepting any single model of classroom research, and for support in the school and within the wider educational context.

Other centres for collaborative inquiry prefer the obverse, i.e. that whatever the problem the method stays the same. The course developed by Elliott for example accepts only naturalistic inquiry based on phenomenology and progressive focusing. In similar vein Connolly and Ben Peretz (1980) reject the notion of the teacher-experimenter arguing that this idea of the 'little researcher' does not lead to improvements in their professionalism. And Bussis (1980) also arguing from a phenomenological standpoint stated that collaboration with practitioners holds enormous potential and can lead to the professional development of teachers if it is linked with ways for teachers to sharpen their capabilities for observation and reflection. However she expresses unease if collaboration turns out in practice to be the training of teachers in the uses of conventional research methods since these equate in her view to 'underlying meaning with test scores'. 'I do not see how training in the reduction of meaning will help them to become better teachers.'

Collaborative inquiry would seem to hold the promise of ensuring practical outcomes of research in schools but to date there have been few evaluation studies. One recent evaluation of the Lancaster initiatives is optimistic however. Silk (1983) concluded, on the basis of interviews with senior school staff, that 'the effect on educational practitioners was well evidenced'. . . . and the extent of that effect appeared to be considerable and to have made an important contribution to the education in those schools. Most got more than they expected, and not always in the predicted, or hoped for, direction. The following quote was typical:

> We got what we wanted and a great deal more. We expected a simple analysis but got many angles on research and not only from the researcher's point of view; children's perspectives, teachers' perspectives; it opened up the whole field. As far as effect is concerned, well, we didn't know how to handle some of the results, they were a bit hot but, as an example, we found it necessary to scrap our induction system and completely re-think our ideas.

One of the major drawbacks to this approach is limitation of application. For every school or teacher involved in such inquiries hundreds are not. However the potential for the wider application of research carried out by teachers could be through the recent increase in teacher fellowships aligned to institutions of higher education. The use made of these fellowships by LEAs is not yet recorded, but those taken up at Lancaster by north-western LEAs are all based on LEA priorities and are used to direct policy decisions. Current examples include the development of LEA priorities in parental participation programmes, the integration of handicapped children into normal schools and curriculum option systems.

The foregoing picture is open to contrasting interpretations. Optimists may perceive those approaches as the genesis of a genuine attempt by researchers to make their research more applied; pessimists may see them as a series of *ad hoc* attempts to make research more relevant. This latter view raises questions about the broader conceptions of applied research in education, particularly with respect to whether this activity can lead to an accumulation of generalizable and usable knowledge of schooling. This broader question, and its implications, are now considered.

Educational Research as an Applied Science

Linking educational research to practice is a venerable aspiration and those who have worked systematically on the articulations of the link (see, for example, Dewey, 1900; Shuell, 1982; Glaser, 1973; Reif, 1978) have perceived the practice of education as an applied science akin in some important respects to engineering, agriculture or medicine. Commentators have pointed with some envy to the achievements of these technologies and in that light have considered education to be in a primitive state of development. However, insofar as such comparisons are useful, it is noteworthy that commentators do not draw attention to the vast resources spent on research informing agriculture or medicine, nor the very large time scale involved in converting basic research findings into useful artefacts, treatments or procedures. For example, the principles of rocketry were known for centuries before space exploration became possible and decades were required to convince medics to wash their hands after treating patients. Also set aside in contemplating the link between research and practice is a recognition of the subtle relationships between the two activities. For example, as Darwin acknowledged, the techniques of selective breeding were known for centuries before he developed his theory of evolution, and the theory in turn has taken decades to influence breeding techniques in ways more profitable than those based on experience.

These reservations are not intended to suggest that there is nothing to learn from applications of work in other fields. Rather, they are intended to moderate the view of what might reasonably be expected over sensible time-scales. This is not the only lesson to be learned from other areas of applied research. Even though the analogy of 'applied science' might not hold as a model for education it is nonetheless possible to identify certain aspects of procedure which, in other areas of human activity such as agriculture or healing, have converted practical wisdom into systematic knowledge. These in turn have provided a foundation for improvements and developments which have enhanced human conditions.

In this respect, Reif (1978) has identified the minimal requirements of an applied science as:

1 The identification of significant problems.
2 An explicit and systematic approach to the collection and validation of a data base.
3 An analysis of the data in terms of theoretical models in an attempt to identify and understand fundamental processes (in this case of schooling).
4 Effective institutional mechanisms for securing the advancement of understanding and for its appropriate utilization.

In the following sections, Reif's specification will be used to identify directions in which improvements might be made. Clearly, the items in Reif's specifications are closely interrelated but are considered separately for ease of exposition.

Neville Bennett and Charles Desforges

The Identification of Significant Problems

All problems are significant to those who have them. Their local or personal significance, however, might be a distraction from more fundamental or general significance. The child's cut knee, finger or head all pose the same problem to a doctor, that of sepsis. But in education we appear to be in a state of egocentrism in the specification of problems. These are often specified for their (frequently short term) political significance or arise out of the pressing interests of minorities or from the vested or particular interests of curriculum groups, for example, the 'reading problem' or the 'science problem', a phenomenon apparent in the earlier sections of this article.

Yet it seems highly likely that more fundamental, and possibly more significant, problems are embedded in these. Thus although research groups in these areas tend to work in isolation it might be predicted that the problems of, for example, learning science, or reading, or mathematics, have, at a fundamental level of analysis, much in common. Despite this each is perceived as a distinct and separate research field.

The danger, particularly at a time of declining resources for research, is that spreading resources over an array of minority or political interests will lead to little long term accumulation of generalizable or usable expertise. Instead the record would show an *ad hoc* collection of problems shot — or at least shot at. What is needed therefore is a systematic examination of research problems in order to identify core areas suitable for concentrating resources on. One implication of this view at the institutional level might be the abandonment of reading or maths centres in favour of the development of teams concerned with the general acquisition of competence.

The Explicit and Systematic Validation of a Data Base

Within the field of education there appears to be little evidence of a progressive accumulation of data. On the contrary it currently seems extremely difficult, if not impossible, to answer questions about the effectiveness of programmes, standards of attainment, quality of learning or the effectiveness of teachers. In part, this may be due to a lack of preliminary conceptual analysis of problems (Wilson, 1972) which leaves data collected open to various interpretations. More frequently it appears to arise from the absence of any explicit statement linking data collected to the problem formulated. HMI reports on schools stand as classic examples of *ad hoc* (and probably extremely expensive) collections of observations on the state of contemporary schooling. The usable implications of these must remain a mystery to the serious minded or an Aladdin's cave to the opportunist.

Serious progress in applications research cannot be expected to rest on 'stories' to which professionals, in their folk wisdom can relate. It will only proceed on the basis of data collected in systematic fashion within a clearly articulated framework which makes it open to public validation.

Identifying and Understanding Fundamental Processes of Schooling

In the past, attempts to apply research and theory have proceeded in ignorance of an understanding of schooling (Desforges, 1981). Little attempt has been made to understand what goes on in the name of schooling, indeed the question has only recently been so boldly put (Olsen, 1976). Whilst many researchers have enthusiastically described what teachers and/or pupils do in school, little effort has been spent in identifying those school processes which account for this behaviour. Condemnation has been more common than comprehension even amongst those who exude humanitarian virtues (see, for example, the work of John Holt or Frank Smith). In developmental terms this can only be described as egocentrism.

Fortunately it is possible to discern some progress in understanding schooling. This is manifest in the work of Doyle (*cf.* 1979, 1983) in the USA for example, and exemplified by Woods (*cf.* 1984). Some important aspects of school life have been formulated within clearly articulated theoretical frameworks and with a commitment to offer testable explanations of particular behaviours. This kind of study is essential to inform implementation work with any hope of success of influencing the central processes of schooling. Without it, applied work is likely to be limited to influencing only peripheral facets of the management of learning.

Although some progress in understanding aspects of schooling are discernable, it is nonetheless the case that significant areas remain a mystery. We have little understanding, for example, of how children learn large bodies of knowledge exemplified in curriculum subjects, nor of what it is they do learn when they are being taught these materials. Yet understanding what children do with available materials seems essential to the design and implementation of potential improvements.

Neville Bennett and Charles Desforges

Effective Institutional Mechanisms for Fostering Applications Research

In a complex system such as institutionalized schooling, the *ad hoc* work of small groups or individuals is unlikely to have any far reaching influence. In the absence of public validation this might, of course, be a saving grace. However, the complexities of the system not only save us from some idiosyncracies, they also stand to bury important and successful ventures and obscure the perceptions of generalizable patterns of progress in understanding and application. It is typically the work of learned societies to foster the growth and dissemination of successful developments.

There appears to be no shortage of societies, institutions or journals. It is simply very difficult to discern their impact. In attempting to improve the effectiveness of research particularly with regard to the longer term accumulation of usable and communicative knowledge perhaps some serious thought needs to be given to these organs. For example, whilst the learned societies in educational research are open to teachers, they appear to have few teacher members. Ideas for developing such active membership might be a suitable subject for a conference symposium.

Conversely the teaching profession itself has shown little commitment to developing a body of professional knowledge and to taking a serious role in communicating this to new members. To initiate interest in this it might be necessary to build research and development work into the teacher's career structure in much the same way as it is in the role of university teachers.

Finally, it must be recognized that few universities have treated educational research and development seriously. This is also true of almost all teacher education institutions outside the university sector. Rather than being actively involved in the business of educational research as a vital part of their teaching programmes they have been content to act largely as transmitters of information. At best they have equipped teachers to be consumers rather than conductors of research.

At the university level a radically new approach would seem to be called for in respect of the collection, collation and systematization of educational knowledge as a foundation on which to base enhanced educational action.

Summary

It has been shown that a variety of modes of applying research to education are being enthusiastically pursued; and although each of these has attendant problems some give grounds for optimism, particularly if judged in terms of the immediate solution to particular problems. However, it has also been argued that serious applications work should show a cumulative record of more generally usable knowledge, and in this respect applied educational research leaves much to be desired.

References

BENNETT, N. (1978) 'Educational research and the media', *Westminster Studies in Education.* 1, pp. 23–30.

BENNETT, S.N. and O'HARE, E. (1980) 'Modes of collaborative research', Paper presented at British Educational Research Association Conference, Cardiff.

BENNETT, S.N., DESFORGES, C.W., COCKBURN, A. and WILKINSON, B. (1984) *The Quality of Pupil Learning Experiences,* London, Lawrence Erlbaum.

BROPHY, J.E. and EVERTSON, C.M. (1974) 'Process-product correlations in the Texas teacher effectiveness study: final report', Research and Development Center for Teacher Education, University of Texas at Austin.

BURDIN, J.L. (1976) 'Realism in research objectives for educational personnel and citizens'. *Journal of Teacher Education,* 27, pp. 1, 2 and 79.

BUSSIS, A.M. (1980) 'Collaboration for what?'. Paper presented at American Educational Research Association Conference, Boston.

CANE, B. and SCHROEDER, C. (1970) *The Teacher and Research.* Slough, National Foundation for Educational Research.

CONNELLY, F.M. and BEN-PERETZ, M. (1980) 'Teachers' roles in the using and doing of research and curriculum development', *Curriculum Studies,* 12, pp. 95–107.

CRAWFORD, J. and STALLINGS, J. (1978) 'Experimental effects of in-service teacher training derived from process-product correlations in the primary grades', Programme on Teaching Effectiveness, School of Education, Stanford University.

DESFORGES, C. (1981) 'Linking theories of cognition and cognitive development to educational practice', Lancaster University, unpublished Ph.D. thesis.

DEWEY, J. (1900) 'Psychology and social practice', *Psychological Review,* 7, pp. 105–124.

DOYLE, W. (1979) 'Making managerial decisions in classrooms', in DUKE D.L. (Ed.), *Classroom Management,* Chicago, University of Chicago Press.

DOYLE, W. (1983) 'Academic work', *Review of Educational Research*, 53, 2, pp. 159–199.

ELLIOTT, J. (1980) 'The teacher as researcher in awardbearing courses', Paper presented at SRHE Conference, London.

EMMER, E.T., SANFORD, J.P., EVERTSON, C.M., CLEMENTS, B.S. and MARTIN, J. (1981) 'The classroom management improvement study: an experiment in elementary school classrooms', Research and Development Center for Teacher Education, University of Texas at Austin.

GAGE, N.L. and COLADARCI, T. (1980) 'Replication of an experiment with a research based in-service teacher education program', Program on Teaching Effectiveness, School of Education, Stanford University.

GAGNE, R.M. (1980) 'Communicating research results to practitioners', Paper presented at the American Educational Research Association Conference, Boston.

GALTON, M., SIMON, B. and CROLL, P. (1980) *Inside the Primary School*, London, Routledge and Kegan Paul.

GLASER, R. (1973) 'Educational psychology and education'. *American Psychologist*, 28, pp. 557–566.

GOOD, T.L. and GROUWS, D.A. (1979) 'The Missouri Mathematics Effectiveness Project: An experimental study in fourth grade classrooms', *Journal of Educational Psychology*, 71, pp. 355-362.

HOUNSELL, D., MARTIN, E., NEEDHAM, G. and JONES, H. (1980) *Educational Information and the Teacher*, Centre for Educational Research and Development, University of Lancaster.

KAY, B. (1977) Letter Introducing DES Policy on Research Funding.

MACKAY, A. (1979) 'Project Quest: Teaching strategies and pupil achievement', *Research Report*, 79–1–3, Centre for Research in Teaching, University of Alberta.

NISBET, J. (1980) in DOCKRELL, W.B. and HAMILTON, D. (Eds.), *Rethinking Educational Research*, London. Hodder and Stoughton.

NIXON, J. (Ed.), (1979) 'Teachers in research', Report of Schools Council Conference, Birmingham.

OLSEN, D. (1976) 'Notes on a cognitive theory of instruction', in KLAHR, D. (Ed.), *Cognition and Instruction*, Hillsdale, N.J., Lawrence Erlbaum Associates.

REIF, F. (1978) 'Toward an applied science of education: Some key questions and directions'. *Instructional Science*, 7, pp. 1–14.

SHUELL, T.J. (1982) 'Developing a viable link between scientific psychology and educational practices'. *Instructional Science*, 11, pp. 155–167.

SILK, E. (1983) 'A Study of the work of the Centre for Educational Research and Development, University of Lancaster', Unpublished M.A. dissertation, Dept. of Educational Research, University of Lancaster.

STALLINGS, J. and KASKOWITZ, D. (1974) 'Follow-through classroom observation evaluation', Menlo Park, California, Stanford Research Institute.

STENHOUSE, L. (1975) *An Introduction to Curriculum Research and Development*, London, Heinemann.

TIKUNOFF, N.J. and WARD, B.A. (1983) 'Collaborative research on teaching', in *Elementary School Journal*, 83, pp. 453–68.

TRAVERS, R.M.N. (1983) *How Research has Changed American Schools,* Kalamazoo, Mythos Press.

WILSON, J. (1972) *Philosophy and Educational Research,* Slough, National Foundation for Educational Research.

WOODS, P. (1985) 'Pupil strategies', in BENNETT S.N. and DESFORGES C. (Eds.), *Recent Advances in Classroom Research,* British Journal of Educational Psychology Monograph, Edinburgh, Scottish Academic Press.

WRIGLEY, J. (1976) 'The impact of educational research', in *SSRC Newsletter,* 32, pp. 3–4.

YATES, A. (Ed.), (1971) *The Role of Research in Educational Change,* Palo Alto, Pacific Books.

Notes on Contributors

CLEM ADELMAN is Research Co-ordinator at Bulmershe College of Higher Education.

PAUL ATKINSON is in the Department of Sociology, University College, Cardiff.

NEVILLE BENNETT is Professor of Education Research, University of Lancaster.

SARA DELAMONT is in the Department of Sociology, University College, Cardiff.

CHARLES DESFORGES is in the School of Education, University of East Anglia.

DENNIS DRYSDALE is Deputy Chief Officer, Further Education Unit and previously Assistant County Education Officer (FE), Isle of Wight County Council.

PETER MITCHELL is in the Institute of Education, London and lately Headteacher, Quinton Kynaston School.

JOHN NISBET is Professor of Education, University of Aberdeen.

MARTEN SHIPMAN is Dean of Education, Roehampton Institute.

EDGAR STONES is Professor Emeritus, University of Liverpool; Honorary Senior Research Fellow in the Institute for Advanced Research in the Humanities, University of Birmingham.

MICHAEL F.D. YOUNG is in the Department of the Sociology of Education, Institute of Education, London.

JACK WHITEHEAD is in the School of Education, University of Bath.

Author Index

Abdullah, M., 104, 107
Abrams, P. *et al.*, 16
Adelman, C., 43n1, 53 and 53n1
   see also Walker and Adelman
Adelman, C. and Gibbs, I., 45
Adelman, C. and Young, M.F.D., 2, 46–55
Adelman, C. *et al.*, 27, 31, 43
Aitkin, M.A., 84
Aitkin, M.A. *et al.*, 61, 70, 84, 95
Anderson, 32
Armstrong, M., 89–90, 96
Atkinson, P., 37, 43
   see also Hammersley and Atkinson
Atkinson, P. and Delamont, S., 2, 14, 26–45
Atkinson, P. and Heath, C., 44
Atkinson, P. and Shone, D., 27, 43 and 43n1

Ball, S.J., 10, 13, 15
Barnes, D., 47, 53
Barnes, D. and Britten, J., 93–4
Barnes, D. *et al.*, 96
Barrett, M., 107
Barton, L., 43n1
   see also Lawn and Barton
Barton, L. and Lawn, M., 36, 37, 43
Barton, L. and Meighan, R., 43
Becker, H., 41–2
Ben Peretz, M.
   see Connolly and Ben Peretz
Bennett, S.N., 10, 15, 48, 50, 51, 52, 53 and 53n4, 61, 70, 83–4, 96, 110, 121

Bennett, S.N. and Desforges, C., 59, 109–23
Bennett, S.N. and O'Hare, F., 114, 121
Bennett, S.N. and McNamara, D., 15
Bennett, S.N. *et al.*, 11, 83, 96, 110, 111, 121
Bernbaum, G., 71
Biklen, S.K.
   see Bogdan and Biklen
Blunkett, D., 73
Bogdan, R. and Biklen, S.K., 11, 15
British Educational Research Association (BERA), 62, 70
Britten, J.
   see Barnes and Britten
Brophy, J.E. and Evertson, C.M., 111, 121
Bruner, J., 87, 89
Bruner, J. *et al.*, 96
Bucuvalas, M.J.
   see Weiss and Bucuvalas
Bulmer, M. and Burgess, R.G., 11, 15
Burdin, J.L., 110, 121
Burgess, R.G., 15
   see also Bulmer and Burgess
Bussis, A.M., 115, 121

Cane, B. and Schroeder, C., 110, 121
Caplan, N., 66, 70
Caplan, N. *et al.*, 66, 70
Carr, W.
   see Kemmis and Carr
Chambers, P., 22, 24

Subject Index

ACC, 73
accountability, 48, 53n3, 114
action research, 97–108
actors
  in research, 47–52
  see also teachers
AERA, 18
AMA, 73
anonymity
  and research, 48–9
anthropology, 30, 31, 35, 38, 39, 46,
  49, 87
APU
  see Assessment of Performance
    Unit
assessment, 92, 93, 114
  see also Assessment of
    Performance Unit
Assessment of Performance Unit
  (APU), 8, 10, 65, 67–8, 92
Association for the Study of the
  Curriculum, 12
Australia
  educational research in, 26
authenticity
  and educational knowledge,
    104–5

Bath, University of, 102
Beachside Comprehensive, 10
behaviourism, 10, 89
BERA
  see British Educational Research
    Association
Beyond the Numbers Game, 31

Birmingham
  inaugural meeting (1974) of
    BERA at, 19
  meeting (1973) on research in
    education at, 18
'bounded system', 29
Bread and Dreams, 30, 33
*Breaking Out: Feminist
  Consciousness and Feminist
  Research*, 14
Britain
  educational research in, *passim*
British Educational Research
  Association (BERA), 9, 12,
    17–25, 94–5
  and classroom studies, 20, 21, 22
  conferences of, 20–1, 23
  constitution of, 19–20
  funding of, 18–20, 21
  membership of, 19–20, 21, 24
  objectives of, 19, 21, 23
  origins of, 17–21
  papers delivered to, 22–3
  presidential addresses to, 22
  publications of, 20–1
  and research workers, 20, 21, 22
  themes considered by, 22–4
*British Educational Research
  Journal*, 21

Burt, Sir Cyril, 12

Callaghan, J., 47
Cambridge Accountability Project,
  12